THE LIFE OF LONGCHENPA

LONGCHEN RABJAM

The Life of Longchenpa

The Omniscient Dharma King of the Vast Expanse

COMPILED AND EDITED BY

Jampa Mackenzie Stewart

INTRODUCTION BY

Yangthang Tulku Rinpoche

SNOW LION
BOSTON & LONDON
2013

Snow Lion
An imprint of Shambhala Publications, Inc.
Horticultural Hall
300 Massachusetts Avenue
Boston, Massachusetts 02115
www.shambhala.com

9 8 7 6 5 4 3 2

Printed in the United States of America

⊗ This edition is printed on acid-free paper that meets
the American National Standards Institute Z39.48 Standard.
♻ This book is printed on 30% postconsumer recycled paper.
For more information please visit www.shambhala.com.

Distributed in the United States by Penguin Random House LLC
and in Canada by Random House of Canada Ltd

Designed by Gopa & Ted2, Inc.

Library of Congress Cataloging-in-Publication Data

The Life of Longchenpa: The Omniscient Dharma King of the
Vast Expanse/Compiled and Edited by Jampa Mackenzie Stewart;
Introduction by Yangthang Tulku Rinpoche. — First edition.
pages cm
ISBN 978-1-55939-418-5 (pbk.: alk. paper)
1. Kloṅ-chen-pa Dri-med-'od-zer, 1308–1363.
2. Rñiṅ-ma-pa lamas—Biography. I. Stewart, Jampa
Mackenzie, 1951– , editor of compilation.
BQ7950.K667L55 2013
294.3'923092—dc23
[B]
2013006446

To Gangteng Tulku Rinpoché, Adzom Paylo Rinpoché, Khen Namdrol Rinpoché, and Yangthang Tulku Rinpoché, my kind teachers, with gratitude for introducing me to the great works and blessings of Longchenpa; to my loving parents, Jim and Natalie Stewart, for their deep goodness, generosity, and support; to Shanti Dechen, my stalwart companion on the path; to my two sons, Adam and Gabriel Stewart; and to all mother beings throughout space.

This book is especially dedicated to all the devoted and dedicated translators upon whom I have relied in the making of this book, and through whose diligent efforts the precious teachings of Tibetan Buddhism are being made accessible to the world.

Equal to the six ornaments of our world and the two supreme ones,
With a spirit of compassion, scriptural understanding, and realization,
Living as a hidden yogi, practicing in forest retreats—
Longchenpa, the perfection of samsara and nirvana as dharmakaya,
Drimé Özer, at your feet I pray.
Fill me with your blessing so that I may realize the natural
state, the essence of my mind.

Since everything is but an apparition,
perfect in being what it is,
having nothing to do with acceptance or rejection, good or bad,
one may well burst out in laughter.

—LONGCHENPA
From *The Natural Freedom of Mind*
(*Semnyi Rangdröl*)*

*Translated by Herbert Guenther in *Crystal Mirror*, vol. 4 (Berkeley, Calif.: Dharma Publishing, 1975), pp. 124–125.

CONTENTS

LIST OF ILLUSTRATIONS

Photo Section

PREFACE

GURU DEVOTION is taught as the highest practice for Tibetan Buddhists. Seeing your teacher as an actual buddha is the swiftest path to enlightenment. And not only your own teacher; a sincere practitioner must arouse true uncontrived devotion to the entire lineage of transmission, from the primordial buddha Samantabhadra down to one's own kind root lama. One needs to arouse faith in the enlightenment of the lineage masters and in their actual attainment of the deepest wisdom and compassion. In this way one can open oneself, become a suitable vessel to receive the inconceivable blessings of the lineage masters.

As the first of the Three Roots, your guru is the root of all blessings. Teachers often quote the saying, "If you see your teacher as an ordinary being, you receive the blessings of an ordinary being. If you see your teacher as a bodhisattva, you receive the blessings of a bodhisattva. If you see your teacher as the buddha, you receive the blessings of a buddha."

So just how does one develop such devotion, this powerful level of faith that can catapult one to awakening? In one's own teacher one naturally responds with faith because the teacher is right in front of one; one sees and hears him or her in the flesh; one can know and be directly moved through one's senses by the amazing field of love and awareness radiating from the actual presence of the body, speech, and mind of the master before one. But what of the lineage masters; what about one's teacher's teacher's teacher; what about those who have passed beyond centuries or millennia ago? How can we feel devotion toward them if they are just names, just figures in a thangka painting, just verses in a lineage prayer?

Aside from meeting them in dreams or visions, one answer is by hearing or reading their personal life story, their spiritual biography or hagiography, what the Tibetans call a "namthar," literally meaning "complete liberation." These are the inspiring tales of beings who started out ordinary and ended up completely awakened to their true nature of mind, the stories of their travails and triumphs on the path that we ourselves are treading. These accounts are easily as vital to us as are the actual teachings and practices. They put a human face on what may seem an abstract experience; they resonate with us as an inspiration that the lofty goal of accomplishment can be accessible to us; they provide us with worthy role models who can serve as a sacred pattern for our lives.

It is therefore an honor to present this compiled biography of the peerless Künkhyen Longchen Rabjampa, commonly known as Longchenpa, the towering fourteenth-century master of Tibet. Although his lifespan of fifty-six years was relatively short, the breadth and depth of Longchenpa's accomplishments and blessings almost defy description. Next to Guru Rinpoché Padmasambhava he is universally recognized as the greatest spokesman on the pinnacle teachings of Tibetan Buddhism: the Great Perfection, Dzogpa Chenpo (or Atiyoga).

The word "prolific" pales in describing his more than three hundred books, practice manuals, sadhanas, and treatises covering the entire spectrum and range of Buddhist teachings and practice. Nearly 650 years after his passing from this world, masters, students, and scholars alike still rely on his written works as the definitive and unmistaken words that bring illumination and clarity to the meaning and intent of Buddha's teachings.

His Eminence Gangteng Tulku Rinpoché, the ninth body emanation of Pema Lingpa, had these words to say about the significance of Künkhyen Longchenpa during a teaching in Crestone, Colorado:

> In Nyingma, Longchenpa is indispensable. His teachings are authoritative works for listening, contemplating, and meditating.
>
> Longchenpa had three incarnations as a tertön. The first was as Pema Ledrel Tsal. The second was as the Omniscient Longchen Rabjam. The third was as the tertön king Pema Lingpa.
>
> Gyalwa Longchenpa is considered an incredibly learned and accomplished master. If one is sectarian, then there is a tendency to be critical of masters from other lineages, saying, "Well, such-and-such a master is learned, but not accomplished," or, "That teacher is learned in sutra, but not in tantra." However, Longchenpa is both accomplished and learned in the sutras and tantras of all the five traditions in Tibet.
>
> Longchenpa's teachings are so thorough, complete, and logi-

cal that there can be no debate about them. So far, no one has really been able to challenge Longchenpa; his position is indestructible. His writings also change the mind of those who read them; they are clearly put forth, in an unerring fashion, and also carry incredible blessings. Longchenpa taught in two ways: the *pandita* way and the *kusali* way. His Seven Treasuries and *Finding Comfort and Ease in the Nature of Mind* (*Semnyi Ngalso*) are presented in the pandita style.

The Dharma protectors Ekajati, Rahula, and Vajra Sadhu (Dorjé Legpa) helped to mix his ink for his many writings, even adding their own blood to the ink! So his teachings are incredibly effective, and the power of his teachings is amazing. Just one *sloka* introduces the experience of the nature of mind.

As an example, Jigmé Lingpa, staying at Forest Charnel Ground at Samyé, had visions of Longchenpa on three different occasions. After receiving his third vision of Longchenpa, his mind dissolved into the vast expanse, and his throat chakra completely unraveled. Even though Jigmé Lingpa wasn't educated, everything was made known to him, and so he was given the title *Künkhyen*, meaning "Omniscient One," because all the teachings were revealed to him.

Many very great recent masters as well, such as Patrul Rinpoché, Jamgön Kongtrul Rinpoché, and Ju Mipham, all received the blessing of mind being resolved into the vast expanse through Longchenpa. So we should open to Longchenpa's blessings, too, have faith, and reflect on his good qualities, and tune in to his great blessing. There is enormous blessing in his teachings, so we should be receptive to that.[1]

Similarly, the great Adzom Paylo Rinpoché, Gyurmé Thubten Gyatso, praises Longchenpa's extraordinary qualities:

There were so many countless prophecies in Buddha's teachings about Longchen Rabjam's coming in the future. Longchenpa was blessed in particular by Guru Rinpoché and Yeshé Tsogyal. Further, because of the way that he approached and served the yidams and completed the practice, he was able to enlist *all* the protectors to aid his aims.

Because Longchenpa had listened so extensively to Buddha's teachings, and had completely accomplished those teachings and become such a vast repository, he was famous in his own time. Through his study, training, and practice under Guru Kumaradza, he gave rise to the four visions of tögal.

Like Manjushri himself, Longchenpa was unrivaled in teaching and debate. He was not only learned, but also accomplished in practice and realization. There was simply no one who could match him.

To illustrate, consider the kindness of Vimalamitra, who said, "In the future, a kind of intellectual faith in Dzogchen will cause decline. To prevent this decline, I will appear in Tibet once every one hundred years." Longchenpa was one of his emanations.

It's astonishing to see the quality and volume of his teaching. He had three nonhuman helpers: [the Dharma protectors] Ekajati, Rahula, and Dorjé Legpa. He composed many works. Even with as many as we still have today, still more of his works have disappeared. All of his works would fill a huge building.

Many great scholars say that the intent of his writings is in accord with Nagarjuna. The way Longchenpa presents the Dharma is not just precise; the words burst forth freshly from his own realization, and so they are endowed with extraordinary blessings. In no way does he transgress Buddha's teachings. He can benefit any level of practitioner, whether through explaining key points or demonstrating the way. Longchenpa can speedily bring about ripening and realization through his teachings.[2]

The great Nyoshul Khenpo expresses his penetrating and unshakeable faith in Longchenpa in the introduction to *A Marvelous Garland of Rare Gems: Biographies of Masters of Awareness in the Dzogchen Lineage* as follows:

Longchenpa embodies all the buddhas and bodhisattvas of the three times and ten directions, all gurus, devas, and dakinis. What we need to realize is the actual meaning of "Longchenpa," which is the essence of what is meant by "being at ease in the nature of mind" (*semnyi ngalso*). It was in order to exemplify and demonstrate that absolute Longchenpa that the omniscient Longchenpa manifested in our world, nearly seven hundred years ago. So by seeing his representation in form, by hearing his speech, and by remembering him, we can receive the blessing that will bring about the realization of the ultimate meaning of Dzogpachenpo. He embodies the intrinsic nature and essence of Dzogpachenpo, which pervades all beings in samsara and nirvana, and so he is never separate from us. All we need to do is to open our hearts in genuine devotion, and his blessing is immediate and utterly within our reach. By praying to Longchenpa, we can awaken the intrinsic, or absolute, Longchenpa within us, the wisdom of our own rigpa, present within the nature of our mind.[3]

In his doctoral dissertation on *The Precious Treasury of Words and Meanings* (*Tshigs don mdzod*), one of Longchenpa's Seven Treasuries, David Germano summarizes Longchenpa's extraordinary significance within the arena of Dzogchen and general Buddhist teachings in Tibet:

> Although at least five hundred years (800 CE–1300 CE) of thought, contemplation and composition in this tradition . . . preceded him such that all the major themes, structures, and terminology were in place prior to his birth . . . it was Longchenpa (1308–1363) who systematically refined the terminology used by the tradition with a series of subtle yet clear distinctions; brilliantly revealed its relationships with mainstream exoteric Buddhist thought; clarified its internal structure; created from it masterpieces of poetic philosophy remarkable for their aesthetic beauty, philosophical rigor, and overall clarity; and overall pinpointed the inner quintessence of the tradition with writings that not only systematized every major topic, but also creatively explained each to render crystal clear the unprecedented revolution in the content, form, and structure of "philosophical" thought in Indo-Tibetan Buddhism that the Great Perfection teachings entail.[4]

As I began to receive teachings and transmissions on Longchenpa's writings from various Tibetan Buddhist lamas, a desire arose in me to find out more about the man behind these incredible works. In doing so, I was astonished to discover that there was no English hagiography presented in one dedicated and comprehensive volume to tell the life story of this extraordinary man, a teacher whose influence on Tibetan Buddhism was both vast and long-lasting.

Fortunately, I was able to find a number of short to medium-length versions of Longchenpa's life appearing within different translated life-story collections of the great Nyingma (Early Translation) School masters. In addition, I have relied on oral teachings from my precious teachers to fill in the details and to shed more light on Longchenpa's great role within Tibetan Buddhism. My intention has been to compile and edit a comprehensive and complete story of the life of Longchenpa for the benefit of the English-speaking world.

The most extensive versions from which I have drawn are in two monumental and historical books: *A Marvelous Garland of Rare Gems: Biographies of Masters of Awareness in the Dzogchen Lineage* by Nyoshul Khenpo, translated by Richard Barron (Chökyi Nyima), and *The Nyingma School of Tibetan Buddhism: Its Fundamentals and History* by Dudjom Rinpoche, Jigdral Yeshe Dorje, translated and edited by Gyurme Dorje and Matthew Kapstein. Both of these works provided extensive details on Longchenpa's life and accomplishments. They are both extraordinary in scope, chronicling the breadth, depth, and scope of the Nyingma lineage and the Dzogchen teachings.

I also found more invaluable biographical information in two works by Tulku Thondup Rinpoche: *Buddha Mind: An Anthology of Longchen Rabjam's Writings on Dzogpa Chenpo* (republished as *The Practice of Dzogchen*) and *Masters of Meditation and Miracles: The Longchen Nyingthig Lineage of Tibetan Buddhism*, both edited by Harold Talbott.

Sarah Harding's translation, *The Life and Revelations of Pema Lingpa*, provided a short but useful biography of Longchenpa, and a rich treasure trove of stories about his previous lives, as well as his future rebirth as the great tertön king Pema Lingpa.

From a terma text, *The Legend of the Great Stupa*, translated by Keith Dowman, I drew the detailed and fascinating story of Longchenpa's earliest known prior lifetime as a bee, whose karmic connections established at that time caused his later rebirth in Tibet in the presence of Guru Rinpoché, known as the Second Buddha.

Wellsprings of the Great Perfection, translated by Erik Pema Kunsang, was another precious source I drew upon; it presents Longchenpa's own version of the history of the Khandro Nyingthig,[5] and the account of how Princess Pemasal, Longchenpa's previous incarnation, came to receive that transmission. This was drawn directly from a translation of Longchenpa's introduction to his work within the collection of the Nyingthig Yabzhi, the *Khandro Yangthig*. I have embellished this account with information from oral teachings received from my lamas.

The Oral Construction of Exile Life and Times of Künkhyen Longchen Rabjam in Bumthang by Dorji Penjore provided rare stories and little-known details about Longchenpa's ten years of self-exile in Bhutan, for which I am most grateful.

In addition, I have included an elegant essay, *In Praise of Longchen Rabjam* by Khenpo Shenga (1871–1927), translated by Adam Pearcey.

I have also excerpted from Yangthang Tulku Rinpoché's precious teachings on Longchenpa's life, his distillation of the Nyingthig teachings of Dzogchen and their inestimable significance for us sentient beings. These were derived from a transcript of the Nyingthig Yabzhi empowerments and teachings given in San Francisco in 1990 (for which I was present), and translated by Sangye Khandro.

Although I have approached this work with the utmost care, I am sure it is not without flaw. For whatever errors or omissions may be discovered in this text I take full responsibility. I warmly invite scholars and practitioners to contact me with suggestions, additions, clarifications, and corrections for use in future editions.

ACKNOWLEDGMENTS

I particularly wish to thank Gangteng Tulku Rinpoché, Adzom Paylo Rinpoché, Yangthang Tulku Rinpoché, and Khen Namdrol Rinpoché, all of whom have a profound lineage connection to Longchenpa, for their teachings on this great man and his precious works. They have been of immeasurable help in cultivating an appreciation for the depth and breadth of Longchenpa's knowledge and attainment and in developing a sense of uncontrived devotion.

I am also grateful to Khenchen Konchog Gyaltshen Rinpoché for helping to clarify some of the historical details about the Drikung monk Künrin's conflict with the king of Tibet, and how this involved Longchenpa; to Lopön Phurba Dorji for providing further details on Longchenpa's time in Bhutan; to Tshering Dorji for clarifying names, places, and cultural details on Bhutan; to Todd R. Gibson for thoroughly reviewing the manuscript and making corrections and valuable suggestions; to Jonathan Landaw for his editorial assistance; to Adam Pearcey for his input on Tibetan language; to Joe Wilson for helping to clarify the meaning and nuances of various Tibetan terms; to Lama Dechen Yeshe Wangmo for helping to shed light on the special meaning of the term *clear light* in the Dzogchen tradition; to Khen Namdrol Rinpoché, Sangye Khandro, Harold Talbott, and Robert and Rachel Olds for their comments on Longchenpa's attainment; to John Loll for his editorial comments; and to Joseph Wagner for his ideas and ongoing encouragement. I give thanks also to Jeffrey Cox and Sidney Piburn of Snow Lion for their enthusiasm and support of the project. Thank you, Nikko Odiseos and to my editors, Steve Rhodes and Liz Shaw, for making this a clearer and more polished read. Thanks also to Robert Beer, Chris Banigan, Ngakchung Rinpoche, Khandro Dechen, Glen Eddy (via his widow Terri Parkin), and Gomchen Oleshey for lending their fine illustrations to adorn this book. And last, but certainly not least, gratitude to my wife and partner, Shanti Dechen, for her encouragement and support of the project, without which none of this would have come to pass.

Finally, I thank all of the precious and extraordinary translators upon whose invaluable work I have relied in the preparation of this book: Sangye Khandro, Lama Chönam Wazi, Keith Dowman, Richard Barron (Chökyi Nyima), Gyurme Dorje, Matthew Kapstein, Tulku Thondup, Harold Talbott, Sarah Harding, Erik Pema Kunsang, Erik Drew, Anne C. Klein, and Adam Pearcey.

May this work of interdependent origination benefit all beings throughout the vastness of space and time.

Jampa Mackenzie Stewart
Crestone, Colorado
Losar, February, 2012
Year of the Male Water Dragon

NOTE ON SANSKRIT AND TIBETAN TERMS

Sanskrit names and words are presented here in phonetic form, without the diacritical marks, to facilitate easier reading.

Tibetan names and words are also, for the most part, presented in phonetic form, without the additional silent consonants.

INTRODUCTION

BY YANGTHANG TULKU RINPOCHE

I N DZOGCHEN there are outer, inner, and secret cycles, and of all of them the Nyingthig is the essence. This is the Dharma that truly brings us the ultimate results in this body. Through this path it is possible to achieve perfect realization in one body and in one lifetime due to the kindness of the great master Longchen Rabjam, or Longchenpa. In our tradition we principally look to Longchenpa, who is the source of the Longchen Nyingthig. His name itself reminds us of the meaning.

The word *longchen* means "vast expanse," which, according to the view of relative truth (which is the external understanding), refers to space that has no limit or boundary and no color or shape. According to the ultimate understanding, or the inner point of view, the word *long*, which means the "expanse," implies "free from any limitation." Specifically, this refers to the four extreme views—existence, nonexistence, both, and neither—and the fact that it has no specific qualities, such as color, form, and so forth; thus, it is the dharmadhatu, the sphere of truth. The word *chenpo* means "great," "the greatest." Because he was one who actualized the view greater than any other—and there will never be another one who actualizes it quite like he did—he is known as "Longchenpa." *Rabjam* means "inconceivable noble qualities," that all of the enlightened qualities of body, speech, and mind have been completely developed, particularly those of knowledge, loving-kindness, and potential. These qualities are inconceivable; it isn't even possible to imagine them. This is the meaning of his name.

The Dzogchen teachings were brought from India to Tibet by the great masters Vimalamitra, Lopön Berotsana,[1] and Guru Rinpoché. After Guru Rinpoché passed to the southwest continent of the *sinpos*,[2] although the Dzogchen doctrine continued to exist in Tibet due to the kindness of those three having established it, it declined to some degree. It was not until later, at the time of Longchenpa, that it was revived and again propagated extensively. It is due to the kindness of Longchenpa, as well as the kindness of Longchenpa's own root guru, the great mahasiddha Kumaradza, and his guru Melong Dorjé, that we have today the pure transmission of the Nyingthig, the Heart Essence.

When Guru Rinpoché came to Tibet he met with Dakini Yeshé Tsogyal. Dakini Yeshé Tsogyal made a great ganachakra feast and one hundred thousand dakinis assembled. Knowing, because of indications, that Guru Rinpoché held the Khandro Nyingthig transmission, Yeshé Tsogyal formally requested that he bestow upon them all the blessing of the Khandro Nyingthig. Guru Rinpoché was very pleased that she had made this request, and he granted her wish. So at this time, to the gathering of hundreds and thousands of dakinis, he revealed the Khandro Nyingthig by way of verbal indication and symbolic indication.

At this same ganachakra feast King Trisong Detsen was present, along with his daughter, Lhacham[3] Pemasal, and it was there that she passed away. At that time Yeshé Tsogyal rose to speak and said that samsara has no essence, that everything is impermanent. Guru Rinpoché also spoke about impermanence, and made many prophecies about future events. Then he wrote the syllable NRI on Lhacham Pemasal's heart, and said her name. Thus he summoned her consciousness back, and she returned to life. Again he gave the empowerment, transmissions, and teachings, and he predicted that, after many lifetimes, this Khandro Nyingthig would be revealed in the world for the benefit of liberating the sentient beings who would have a karmic affinity with it at that time. Many lifetimes later Lhacham Pemasal was reborn as Longchenpa, and it was Longchenpa who revealed the transmissions of the Khandro Nyingthig.

As for the Vima Nyingthig, when Guru Rinpoché was at Samyé Monastery with King Trisong Detsen, they invited five hundred of the greatest Indian panditas to come. Of all of these, Vimalamitra was considered to be the greatest. When he came to Tibet, he brought the teachings of the Clear Light Atiyoga[4] and bestowed upon Guru Rinpoché and the twenty-five disciples the teachings of the Zabmo Nyingthig—the profound teachings in the Nyingthig cycle—and many other teachings. These teachings were then buried as termas. Vimalamitra later went to China, to the Riwo Tsé-Nga, the Five-Peaked Mountain,[5] and he died there. At the time of his passing, he prophesied that he would be reborn each hundred years, and he was later reborn as Longchenpa.

VIMALAMITRA

So, while Longchenpa is well known to be the emanation of Pemasal, King Trisong Detsen's daughter, he is also considered to be an emanation of Vimalamitra. Thus, in his compiling of the Vima Nyingthig, because he is an emanation of Vimalamitra this material comes out of his own mind— some are the very termas he revealed as Vimalamitra. In fact, if one should want to receive the teachings that Vimalamitra presented in Tibet, they can all be found in the Vima Nyingthig; nothing is missing. Furthermore, because there had been some breaking and deterioration of the samaya with the passage of time, Longchenpa, knowing this, revealed these works again. He then revised them, recollected them, and made a new version. So we can consider this new version of Longchenpa's to be the most authentic.

Longchenpa's guru was the great mahasiddha Kumaradza, and Kumaradza's guru was Melong Dorjé. All of these gurus were masters of the highest Dzogchen realization; they accomplished nothing less than the rainbow body. Literally, they dissolved their bodies into clear light. Such is the power of the Nyingthig doctrine.

Longchenpa is the owner, or holder, of the Nyingthig. He actually received it from his teacher, Kumaradza, who gave him the entire Nyingthig teachings without exception.

From Vimalamitra all the way to Longchenpa, and even up to our present time, there is an unbroken chain of lamas who have achieved the highest realization, the rainbow body, and nothing less. Some of them accomplished the rainbow body without traces. When they passed, their bodies simply dissolved into light molecules, and they were gone to the pure realms without leaving a single trace of a corporeal form behind. Some of them passed away leaving only their hair and nails behind. And at the passing of others, due to their realization, a tremendous vibration of sound came from all directions of space, the earth shook, relics manifested from their bodies, and many other inconceivable signs occurred. My own lama achieved the rainbow body in Tibet; this I saw with my own eyes.

You should have no doubt that this type of achievement is possible through the power of this practice. Perhaps the deciding point is nothing other than one's own diligence. If you are diligent, you too will achieve the rainbow body, you too will have these kinds of signs. You won't need to pass through the bardo. You won't need to be born again in the three realms of cyclic existence.[6] When you die, relics will manifest from your body. The Nyingthig gives us this type of great blessing. Truly, the Dharma is something you need not doubt, and with this type of Dharma you should never have a single moment of doubt about its power—but you must be diligent. You must know how to exert yourself in practice with enthusiastic effort, especially since it is at this time you have achieved the precious human rebirth so difficult to achieve. Having met with this type of powerful doctrine, if you are not diligent now, when will such an opportunity come again? Now is the time to try to get out of the three realms of cyclic existence so that you will no longer have to experience suffering. You have to try.

In this way the blessings of Longchenpa are truly inconceivable. Beyond all trace of doubt, he is the true holder of the Nyingthig. For practitioners of Dzogchen, he is our unmistaken object of supplication. He is incomparable. He was authorized again and again by Guru Rinpoché and Vimalamitra, who continued to appear to him to give him spiritual authorization and authority. All of these emanations told him that, more than any other Dzogchen lama, he is the greatest. Surely, if we supplicate him, we will not be mistaken.

THE LIFE OF LONGCHENPA

PADMASAMBHAVA

PRELUDE

This is an excerpt from *The Legend of the Great Stupa*, a terma treasure of Padmasambhava. It reveals the story of the first known lifetime of Longchenpa.

Translated by Keith Dowman[1]

THIS IS THE history of Jarungkhasor, the Great Stupa, which is the receptacle of the dharmakaya, which is identical to the mind of all buddhas and bodhisattvas of the three times and the ten directions. In the year of the fire-male-monkey on the tenth day of the monkey month, in the middle chamber of the great monastery Samyé Ling, which means "the inconceivable, unchanging, and spontaneously arisen," when the great religious king Trisong Detsen and twenty-five disciples of the Guru were assembled to receive initiation into the *Innermost Secret Mind of the Lama*,[2] Orgyen Rinpoché, the precious Lotus-Born Guru of Orgyen, was asked to remain seated on his throne of nine piled cushions. Then King Trisong Detsen offered his Guru a golden chalice of wine, various delicacies to eat gathered from all over the world, twenty-one turquoises drawn from the necklace which hung from his own neck, five cups of gold, seven bowls of gold, eight clothes of fine silk, and a vast store of other riches.

Prostrating before his Guru one thousand times, the king addressed him, "O Great Guru! I was born in Tibet, this barbarian country of red-faced monkeys, and I invited the sage bodhisattva Shantarakshita from the country of Zahor and you, the Abbot of Orgyen, the Lotus-Born Guru, to establish the Dharma in this country. I have built the great monastery of Samyé wherein resides the Triple Gem, the receptacle of the accumulated merit of all beings, incomparable throughout the southern world of Jambudvipa. I have achieved these things. Now, in this barbarian country which is like an island of darkness, the doctrine of the Triple Gem is diffusing like the early morning sun of the mountain peaks and all people can hear the explanation of the holy religion as they did in the Golden Age when Mahakashyapa Buddha taught in the central land of Magadha.

"When Mahakashyapa Buddha was preaching, the benefactress Jadzima, who begat four sons, built the Jarungkhasor Stupa in the district of Maguta, in the kingdom of Nepal. Great Guru! If you could speak to us of the fruit of the aspiration generated by the builders of that first Great Stupa, then we, having built this great monastery of Samyé, knowing how to pray, may become full of confidence and faith in the future. So that we may be devoted, we entreat you to describe in detail the result of building that first Great Stupa of Jarungkhasor."

Then the Great Guru spoke in reply, "O Great King, listen carefully and remember my words! I will relate to you the legend of Jarungkhasor. In a bygone age countless kalpas ago, the bodhisattva mahasattva, the Lord Avalokiteshvara vowed at the feet of his guru, the Buddha Amitabha, to liberate all beings from the misery of this world. Then having delivered innumerable beings from sorrow, he climbed to the top of the Potala Palace, thinking that all beings without exception had been released. But looking over the six realms he saw many beings still languishing in the lower worlds like flies on a refuse heap. Thinking that it was not possible to deliver all beings from the ocean of misery which is this world, he wept, and, wiping two teardrops from his eyes with his forefinger, he prayed that even these two tears might assist beings of the future to overcome their sorrow. In fulfillment of that prayer those two teardrops were transmuted and incarnated as two daughters of King Indra, who resided in the Heaven of the Thirty-three Gods. The daughters were named Goddess Purna (Complete) and Apurna (Incomplete). Apurna once stole some flowers, and as a punishment for violating the law of the gods she was reborn in the human world, in the country of Nepal in the district of Maguta, to a poultryman, Ansu, and his wife, Purna. She was named the poultrywoman Shamvara. When she matured she copulated with four different men, all of low caste, and bore a son by each of them. The first son was born of a stablehand, the second of a swineherd, the third of a dog keeper, and the fourth of a poultryman.

"The poultrywoman Shamvara amassed sufficient wealth from her business to rear her sons well and to establish them as educated householders. Later she accumulated much wealth from her profits and then thought to herself, 'My savings from the poultry business have permitted me to establish my sons as respectable householders. Now I have accumulated a further

KING TRISONG DETSEN

store of wealth, and so that all men may benefit from it, I shall build a Great Stupa, a receptacle for the mind of all the buddhas, my own projected divinity. It shall be a place of adoration for innumerable beings, and a reliquary for the indestructible remains of the tathagatas. But first I must ask the permission of the Maharaja.'

"Then having thought within herself in this manner, she approached the Maharaja, prostrated herself before him, circumambulated him, knelt down before him, placed her palms together and appealed to him, 'O Great King! I am a poor woman, a poultrywoman, and single-handedly I have raised four sons of different fathers with the profit of my business and established them as householders. I crave your permission to build a Great Stupa which will be my projected divinity, which will be a place of adoration for innumerable beings, which will be a receptacle of the mind of all the buddhas, and which will be a reliquary for the indestructible remains of the tathagatas. It will be constructed with the wealth that I have accumulated since my sons became self-sufficient.'

"A great king never makes hasty decisions. The King composed his mind for a moment and pondered within himself, 'This poultrywoman is a poor woman who has saved sufficient wealth to bring up four illegitimate sons and now she wishes to build a Great Stupa. This is wonderful and amazing.'

"Then he gave her permission to build the stupa. The poultrywoman Shamvara was filled with contentment and joy, and again prostrating before the king, circumambulated him many times and returned home. Then the construction of the Great Stupa was begun by the woman, her four sons, an ass, and an elephant. Earth was brought to the site, foundations were laid, and walls were built up to the third level. It was at this time that the people of Nepal came together, feeling full of resentment towards the poultrywoman who had shamed them by her superior achievement, and asked each other what sort of construction should be expected of the king, the minister, the wealthy, and the famous if a poor poultrywoman could build such a stupa. Considering themselves insulted and injured, they went to the king with a petition to obstruct the work. They said to him, 'O Great King! You have blundered. If this poor poultrywoman can construct such a Great Stupa, what should be expected of you, the King, the ministers, and the wealthy men of the country? If you permit this construction, every one of us will be humiliated. It would be better if the earth and stones were carried back to the quarry. It is not proper that she be permitted to build this stupa.'

"The Great King replied to them, 'Listen to me carefully! This poor poultrywoman has saved sufficient riches to bring up four illegitimate sons and has accumulated sufficient wealth to build this stupa. I consider this a marvelous achievement. I have already given her my permission to proceed with the work. I, being a king, speak only once.'

"Other men also tried to obstruct the progress of the construction, but unsuccessfully. So the Great Stupa became known as Jarungkhasor,³ which means that once authority to build has been given, every obstacle can be overcome. The work of construction continued without interruption throughout summer and winter for four years until the stupa was completed up to the neck.

"But at that time the poor poultrywoman, discovering that she was dying, called her four sons and their servant to her and said, 'Complete this Great Stupa, which is my projected divinity, and which is the place of adoration for both mundane and supramundane beings. Place the indestructible remains of the tathagatas within this stupa and then consecrate it with great honor and reverence. This is my wish, and when it is fulfilled, the grand intentions of all the buddhas of the past, present, and future will be realized. And you, my sons, will also fulfill the purpose of this life and the next by obeying my wishes.'

"With these words she passed away. Cymbals sounded and the gods sent a rain of flowers; many rainbow lights shone in the sky, and the poor poultrywoman Shamvara, through her generosity in constructing the Great Stupa, attained buddhahood and was called Chamsi Lhamo Pramsha. The four sons remaining faithful to their mother's wish, to repay her kindness to them and attain merit, agreed to complete the stupa and add the upper portions. So, as before, the sons loaded bricks upon the elephant and donkey and continued the work. They worked for three more years before the construction was completed; seven years in all. The indestructible remains of the Tathagata Mahakashyapa (the Buddha of the previous age) were sealed in the tree of life within the stupa.

"Then after sumptuous offerings had been arranged and consecrating flowers strewn everywhere, the Tathagata Mahakashyapa, surrounded by his attendant bodhisattvas, appeared throughout the fields of the sky in front of the stupa. All the buddhas and bodhisattvas of the ten directions, with innumerable arhats surrounding them, the five lineages of tathagatas, the Lords of the Three Worlds, and the innumerable wrathful and peaceful deities beyond conception like blooming buds of sesame appeared there, scattering flowers, honoring the occasion with their most auspicious presence.

Many cymbals sounded, and the gods sent a storm of flowers, while sweet-smelling incense wafted in every direction. The earth itself shook three times. The boundless light of divine wisdom diffusing from the bodies of the assembled tathagatas eclipsed the sun and irradiated the night for five consecutive days."

Again King Trisong Detsen spoke to the Lotus-Born Guru, "O Great Guru! I entreat you to describe the prayers that were offered and the aspirations that were formed before this most marvelous stupa called Jarungkhasor, and relate to us the story of the fulfillment of those prayers."

The Great Guru replied, "Listen to me, O Great King! When flowers were scattered at the consecration of the stupa, and when fantastic miracles were performed and wonderful sights were seen, the vast assembly of buddhas and bodhisattvas addressed the benefactors with one voice and said, 'Listen, O you most fortunate and well born! Through the pure mind which created the wish to construct this Great Stupa, the supreme receptacle of the dharmakaya, which is inseparable from the mind of all the victorious ones of the past, present, and future, through this benefaction whatever prayer you offer will be granted in perfection.'

"Then the sons of the deceased poultrywoman said to each other, 'It was the enlightened vow of our old mother that led to the construction of this stupa, but following her deathbed wishes we completed the edifice and consecrated it and were privileged to see the countenance of all the buddhas and bodhisattvas. Now, through that accumulated merit, we may ask for the fulfillment of any prayer; it would be unwise to pray for any petty thing.'

"The eldest son, the son of a stablehand, considered what universal prayer he could offer: 'In the icebound and barbarous kingdom to the north the mountains are snow covered and the valleys are flooded; it is the haunt of waterbirds in summer, and it is one vast ice field in winter. It has been prophesied that the floods will subside and that after the bodhisattva, Lord of the Universe, Avalokiteshvara has come to train the inhabitants in the lore of the Tathagata Shakyamuni, the doctrine of the buddhas will be diffused throughout the land. It is my prayer that I may establish the doctrine of the buddhas in Tibet.'

"So he prayed accordingly: 'Through the merit that I have won in completing this stupa with pure heart and aspiration may I be born as a great king and protector of religion in the icebound border country of savages to the north. When the power of the five poisons—hatred, lust, sloth, jealousy, and pride—increases in the Kaliyuga, the time of destruction and corruption, spreading the lore of the Tathagata Shakyamuni, may I establish the doctrine of the buddhas there for all time.'

"The second son, the son of the swineherd, then offered his prayer: 'Through the merit that I have won in completing the Great Stupa, when my brother has been reborn as a king and protector in the icebound land of savages and when the precious doctrine of the Buddha is being established, and the necessity arises to introduce the community of the Sangha, the foundation of the doctrine, into that country, may I be reborn as a bhikshu who will become a great arhat to ordain converts as members of the Sangha.'

"Then the third son, the son of the dog keeper, offered this prayer: 'Through the merit that I have won in completing this stupa, when my two brothers have established the doctrine of the buddhas in the icebound land of savages, and when the people follow the doctrine of the buddhas, may I be born not from a woman's womb but miraculously from the pollen bed of a lotus. Destroying the succession of life and death, may I live as long as the sun and moon. Subduing and training gods, demons, and men alike and subjecting all the poisonous cannibal natives of that barbarous country, may I be reborn as a tantric yogin, a mantra holder, to guard the buddhas' doctrine which my brothers will establish.'

"Then the youngest son, the son of the poultryman, offered this prayer: 'Through the merit that I have won in completing this stupa, when you three have been reborn in the icebound land of savages, one to establish the doctrine, one to keep it steadfast, and one to guard it, may I be born as the minister who will coordinate your activities.'

"After the four sons had offered their prayers, all the buddhas and bodhi-sattvas spoke to them with one voice: 'O worthy sons! Most fortunate beings! You have offered truly exalted and unselfish prayers. All the buddhas are rejoicing with you. The mountain of merit that you have produced by this prayer is incomparable—even the buddhas of the three times are unable to match it.'

"Then all the buddhas of the ten directions and all the bodhisattvas dissolved in a single flash of light which vanished into the Great Stupa. Thereafter the stupa became known throughout the world as the 'Unity of Buddhas.'

"Just then, a bee settled on the stablehand's son's neck and stung him, causing intolerable pain. This led him to brush off the insect with his hand, killing it. But with boundless compassion he prayed in this way: 'When I am born as a religious king in the icebound land of the savages, may this insect be reborn as a prince practicing Dharma.'

ABBOT SHANTARAKSHITA

". . . In this way, at this time, innumerable prayers were offered to benefit all beings and all these boundless prayers were granted. The eldest son, the stablehand's son who prayed for rebirth as a king, has been reborn as you, yourself, King and Protector of Religion, Trisong Detsen! The swineherd's son, who prayed for rebirth as an abbot, has been reborn as the Abbot and bodhisattva Shantarakshita. The dog keeper's son, who prayed to be reborn as a tantric yogin, has become myself, the Abbot of Orgyen, the Lotus-Born Guru. The poultryman's son, who prayed for rebirth as a religious minister, is the present king of Yarlung. The bee for whom rebirth as a prince had been supplicated is the present princess Pemasal. . . ."

The Lotus-Born Guru ceased speaking. The King Trisong Detsen and the whole assembly were amazed and credulous. They prostrated themselves again and again before offering powerful prayers for the doctrine and for all sentient beings.

SAMAYA GYA GYA GYA   SEAL THE THREEFOLD BOND

Samantabhadra/Samantabhadri Yab-Yum

1. His Previous Lives

***

Know the state of pure and total presence to be a vast expanse,
without center or border; it is everywhere the same, without
acceptance or rejection. Blend the nature of mind
and its habit patterns into nonduality.
—Longchenpa*

L ONG AGO, in the very beginning, way before there were even the names
"samsara" and "nirvana," when, in fact, neither of these two distinctions
even existed, there was Kuntuzangpo *yab-yum*, one's own nature, which is
nothing other than the state of perfected buddhahood. And dwelling in
that originally pure awareness nature were the six specific dharmas of Dzogchen,[1] the display of that pure awareness, which are the five buddhas and
their consorts dwelling in the dharmakaya, and the manifestations of Vajrasattva as the sambhogakaya. The realization of the nature of the mind, of
that which is Kuntuzangpo, was naturally self-originating as Vajrasattva
through the blessing of the manifestation of the body, speech, and mind of
enlightened awareness. Not a single word was necessary. Vajrasattva simply
self-originated with all of the blessings of the original nature as the display
of that nature.

Then Vajrasattva appeared in the blazing charnel grounds to the nirmanakaya Garab Dorjé, and by way of verbal indication he gave these teachings of the pure awareness nature, the perfected nature, to Garab Dorjé.
Thus, Garab Dorjé is considered to be the human being who opened the
door to the Atiyoga in this world.

Then, by way of direct introduction to the dharmata, Garab Dorjé passed
the teachings on to Lopön Shri Singha. In that transmission the pure aware-

* Translated by Kennard Lipman and Merrill Peterson in *You Are the Eyes of the World,* p. 42.

GARAB DORJÉ

ness nature was directly perceived at the very instant it was introduced. Lopön Shri Singha then passed this introduction on to Lopön Padmasambhava, Guru Rinpoché. This transmission took place by way of just remaining in the fundamental nature as it is, without a single thought, idea, or any aspect of mental activity, free from mental fabrications entirely. In that state of awareness it was passed directly into the mind of Guru Rinpoché.[2]

Now during this time, in the Tibetan border area of Chokro Dri, and in the great region of the Kharchen clan, a chieftain named Tokar Lek of Mangjé married Lady Gyamo Tso of Ru, a woman of the Nup clan. After their marriage, one night Lady Gyalmo Tso dreamed that a blue woman appeared in the middle of the sky emitting light; the woman threw a radiant star that entered into Gyalmo Tso's womb. Soon after, Gyalmo Tso knew that she was pregnant.

After nine months and ten days, Gyalmo Tso gave birth to a very beautiful baby girl who had the mark of a crossed vajra on her forehead, and whose body gave off the fragrance of a blue lotus flower. Her parents named the lovely girl Tsogyal, Lake of Victory, because the lake by their home increased in size at the hour of her birth. It can still be seen today at Tsogyal Latso in Central Tibet.

When Tsogyal grew up, she was accepted by King Trisong Detsen as a queen of Tibet. Due to her great faith and deep devotion to the Lotus-Born Guru Padmakara and her disenchantment with samsara, she begged the king for permission to practice the Dharma. King Trisong Detsen agreed, and offered her to Guru Rinpoché, who took her as his consort. She followed him wherever he went, honoring him and serving him. She pursued her practice so one-pointedly that she attained great accomplishment of both the ordinary and supreme siddhis. She now became known as Yeshé Tsogyal, Wisdom Lake of Victory.

Later, at a time when the master and his consort were practicing in the Tidro Cave at Upper Zho, the wisdom dakinis of timeless awareness all exhorted the noble lady Tsogyal, saying, "This great master, this nirmanakaya emanation, holds in his heart the profound transmission of the Nyingthig teachings of direct experience, the teaching through which one awakens to enlightenment within three years, so that in this very lifetime one's material body vanishes. You *must* beseech him to give you these teachings." Thus she received the directions of the dakinis.

So, Yeshé Tsogyal presented a lavish feast offering, and then made her request to Guru Rinpoché, saying, "Great master, I humbly ask that you bestow upon me the sacred and profound pith instructions of the Nyingthig teachings of direct experience, the teaching on awakening to enlightenment within three years so that the material body vanishes in this very lifetime." With this supplication, she made innumerable prostrations and circumambulations.

In response, the great master replied, "Tsogyal, your request is an excellent one. This instruction is really unlike any other that you have requested before, and unlike any that I have given in the past. It is the pinnacle of all the nine spiritual approaches. By seeing its key point, intellectually created views and meditations are shattered; the paths and levels are perfected without any need for effort; negative emotions are liberated in their own place without any need for correction or antidote. This teaching brings one to perfect realization, the fruition that is not created by causes. It instantly

DAKINI YESHÉ TSOGYAL

brings forth spontaneously present enlightenment; within this very lifetime one's material body of flesh and blood is liberated as the luminous sambhogakaya, a state of pure lucidity; and it enables you to capture, within three years, in the domain of Akanishtha, the ongoing state of genuine being in the pure dharmakaya realm of spontaneous presence. I possess such an instruction, the Khandro Nyingthig, and I shall teach it to you."

Having spoken these words, Padmasambhava then revealed the ultimate mandala of the peaceful and wrathful deities in the great assembly hall of the dakinis at Tidro Cave in Upper Zho, and bestowed the empowerment on one hundred thousand wisdom dakinis, headed by the bride of the Kharchen clan, Yeshé Tsogyal as foremost amongst them, and also to King Trisong Detsen and Vairotsana. The guru did so by placing his right hand on the head of the king, his left hand on the head of Vairotsana, and touching his head to the head of Yeshé Tsogyal, whispered these highest teachings to them.[3]

Having given the complete instructions and empowerment, he then taught the Seventeen Tantras as well as the eighteenth, the *Tantra of the Sun of the Brilliant Clear Expanse of Samantabhadri,* and gave many pith instructions based on these tantras. Of these, the pith instructions that elaborated on the themes of the extensive tantras were gathered into one category, while the *kusali*[4] cycles for yogis, written by the guru himself, were compiled into another. These were separately classified and recorded by both Guru Padmasambhava and Yeshé Tsogyal and entered into a list of contents. Having been classified and recorded, Guru Padmasambhava then conferred the empowerment for them, along with the seal of his aspirations and entrustment.[5]

Around this time, at the invitation of King Trisong Detsen, Guru Rinpoché and Yeshé Tsogyal went up to the sacred site of Samyé Chimphu[6] and participated in 108 feast offerings. Also present at the feast were Guru Rinpoché's twenty-five close disciples, along with King Trisong Detsen, his queens, and his offspring, including his eight-year-old daughter, Princess Pemasal.[7]

Princess Pemasal had been born to one of King Trisong Detsen's queens, the beautiful Lady Dromza Jangchub Men. She was devoted to the Dharma and to Guru Rinpoché from the time she was five years old, and was also bright beyond her years. Because of this, she was allowed to receive many profound transmissions and teachings of the outer and inner tantras. In particular, the little princess learned *The Union of Samantabhadra's Intent,*[8] *Lama Jewel Ocean,*[9] *The Great Compassionate One: The Lamp That Dispels the Darkness,*[10] and other teachings as well. In a short time, through the blessings of the guru, this special young girl was actually able to recognize primordial purity of intrinsic awareness, the true nature of mind.

It was in the midst of this ganachakra feast, high in the mountains around Chimphu, that Princess Pemasal was suddenly stricken by spasmodic dysentery, a parasite, and passed away without any warning. When he saw his beloved daughter's dead body, her father King Trisong Detsen was beside himself with shock and grief, and fell to the ground weeping.

Yeshé Tsogyal took a white silk cloth and sprinkled him with saffron water. When the king had regained his senses, Guru Rinpoché spoke: "Listen, your majesty.

PRINCESS PEMASAL

In general, all worldly pursuits are like dreams.
The mark of composite things is that they are like magical illusions.
Your kingdom itself is like last night's dream.
Your wealth and subjects are like dew drops on a blade of grass.
This fleeting life is like bubbles upon water.
All composite things will perish.
All meetings end in parting.
All composite things are like this.
There is not one thing that is stable and lasting.
Don't cling to the impermanent as if it were permanent.
Train in the nonarising nature of dharmakaya.

Thus he spoke.

The king made many prostrations and circumambulations, and then said,
"Great master, since samsaric pursuits are futile, please give me a teaching for being content in this life, happy in the following life, and ultimately awakening to enlightenment."

Again the master spoke to the king:

Emaho!
Your majesty, great king, listen once more!
Since samsaric things have no essence,
To continue endlessly spinning about brings further and further
    suffering,
So capture the royal stronghold of dharmakaya.

As your true homeland, keep to the nonarising dharmadhatu.
As your true dwelling, adhere to forest retreats and remote places.
As your true retreat, look into the empty and luminous dharmata.
As your true house, remain in your original mind nature.

As your true bounty, keep attentive and mindful.
As your true treasury, form the resolve of the twofold awakened mind.
As your true wealth, keep to the two accumulations.
As your true farming, endeavor in the ten virtuous practices.

As your true fatherhood, embrace all beings with compassion.
As your true motherhood, sustain the natural state of emptiness.

As your true offspring, practice development and completion
    indivisibly.
As your true spouse, train in bliss, clarity, and nonthought.

As your true companion, read the scriptures of the sugatas.
As your true farm land, cultivate unshakeable faith.
As your true food, eat the nonarising nectar of dharmata.
As your true beverage, drink the nectar of oral instructions.

As your true clothing, wear the garment of modesty and decorum.
As your true retinue, preserve the dakinis and protectors.
As your true enjoyment, engage in spiritual practice.
As your true spectacle, look into your own mind.

As your true diversion, engage in elaborate spiritual pursuits.
As your true entertainment, train in emanating and absorbing,
    the development stage.
As your true close friend, keep to the empowerments and samayas.
As your true prejudice, use the five poisons for training.

As your true ornament, study and reflect free from partiality.
As your true activity, have the profound scriptures copied.
As your true caller, be generous without bound.
As your true pursuit, direct your innermost aim to the Dharma.

As your true court chaplain, venerate the Three Jewels.
As your true objects of respect, treat your parents with reverence.
As your true object of honor, respect your vajra master.
As your true samaya, keep your mind free from hypocrisy.

As your true precept, give up all evil.
As your true temple, keep the three precepts purely.
As your true mandala, look into the unchanging luminosity.
As your true instruction, tame your own mind.

As your true view, look into the changeless, empty cognizance.
As your true meditation, let your mind nature be as it is.
As your true conduct, let the delusion of dualistic fixation collapse.

As your true fruition, don't seek the result that is spontaneously
   present.

If you practice like this, you will be content in this life, joyful in
   the next,
And soon attain complete enlightenment.

On hearing this song, the king was delighted, and made many prostrations and circumambulations. Then, again overcome by the sudden loss of
his beloved and special young daughter, the king beseeched Guru Rinpoché
for his help with tears streaming from his eyes.

Padmasambhava then placed the pith instructions and the brocade cloak
that had belonged to the princess inside a brown chest of rhinoceros hide,
and concealed it as a terma treasure with the wish that the princess meet
with it again. He then knelt down beside the still, dead body of the little
girl, and with his finger wrote the sacred syllable NRI over Princess Pemasal's
heart in vermillion, and spoke her name. Miraculously, he summoned her
consciousness back into her body with the hook of his compassion, and
within moments she returned to life, breathing deeply and opening her eyes,
once again alive and able to speak.

King Trisong Detsen was still perplexed as to why his daughter had died
so young. He asked Guru Rinpoché why this was happening.

Guru Rinpoché replied, "She is not the product of high aspiration.
When we were building the Great Stupa in Nepal, I, Guru Rinpoché, you,
King Trisong Detsen, and Abbot Shantarakshita were brothers. You, King
Trisong Detsen, slapped and killed a bee, who is reborn now as your daugh-
ter, Princess Pemasal, due to your pure prayers of aspiration for the bee at
that time. This explains the karmic connection."

Still weak from her near-death experience and illness, Princess Pemasal
asked softly, "What will I be in my future lives?"

Guru Rinpoché replied, "At first, you will have three lesser rebirths. After
that, you will have three pure births as a great tertön. The first will be as
Pema Ledrel Tsal; the second, as Longchen Rabjam; and the third will be
as the tertön king Pema Lingpa. In your life as Pema Lingpa you will hold
the key to 108 mind termas."

Princess Pemasal then asked Guru Rinpoché, "Please give me a practice
that is easy to learn, easy to use, easy to understand, with few words, and that
will lead to full enlightenment easily."

Knowing that Princess Pemasal was going to die very soon, and that it is very hard to prevent karma at the ripening stage, he said, "These teachings have been hidden in my heart. Truly you do not have long to live, and have many obstacles, so you will require some especially potent teachings." And so he gave her the transmissions of the Khandro Nyingthig, the essence of the secret treasury of Dzogchen, like having the Buddha in the palm of your hand.

He also gave her the secret name of Pema Ledrel Tsal. She then placed the casket containing the Khandro Nyingthig teachings on her head and spoke the following aspiration prayer: "At some time in the future may I meet again with these teachings and bring benefit to beings." Princess Pemasal and Yeshé Tsogyal then wrote the texts down on yellow silk with blood from Yeshé Tsogyal's nostrils.

Master Padmasambhava explained that when the karma of the former life of the princess reawakens, she will meet again with her father, brothers, and the master himself. He then allowed her spirit to pass on, and acted as if performing the funeral ceremony at that same place. But in order to purify her obscurations he brought her dead body in an instant to Oddiyana and performed a feast offering.

In an instant he returned, and said, "Tsogyal, write these events down in a narration. Conceal them, together with the profound terma treasure. By doing so, when she meets it in the future, she will believe in it."

So Lady Tsogyal committed this to writing, then asked the master, "Should these instructions on the Secret Heart Essence be propagated or concealed?"

The master replied, "The time has not yet come for them to be propagated, so they should be concealed as a terma treasure. The princess made an aspiration when I placed the casket with the text at the crown of her head, and therefore the teachings will be her heritage. Some years from now, the great master Vimalamitra will arrive and, since the time will have come for his disciples, the teachings of the Heart Essence will flourish.

"When the early translations have become corrupted so that they are close to perishing, and the Buddhadharma is about to disappear, these teachings of my Khandro Nyingthig will manifest widely and forcefully, but briefly, just like the flame of a butter lamp flares up before burning out.

"In general, the teachings of the Old School will be widespread but short-lived, and among them the terma teachings especially will flourish at the same time as the terma door opens. They will for the most part subside when the destined owner of the terma remains no longer. Therefore, conceal these teachings."

And so he predicted that, after many lifetimes, this Khandro Nyingthig and other precious termas would be revealed in the world at the appropriate time by future rebirths of Princess Pemasal for the benefit of sentient beings. He recorded these events, and asked Dakini Yeshé Tsogyal to help him conceal these teachings as termas for future followers.

Then Guru Rinpoché and Yeshé Tsogyal themselves concealed the teachings in two different places. The extensive eighteen tantras and elaborate teachings of the Learned Pandita cycle were hidden at Long-Nosed Lion Cliff[11] in the lower Bumthang area of what is now Bhutan (then known as Mönyül), while the profound condensed kusali teachings of the Khandro Nyingthig and tantras were hidden at the Overhanging Cave at the Multicolored Cliff of Danglung Tramo Drak in Dakpo Valley.

Many dakas and dakinis appeared in the sky, and Guru Rinpoché entrusted the texts to them, and to the dharmapalas Dza Rahula, Mamo Ekajati, and Dorjé Legpa, who were sworn by Guru Rinpoché to give the teachings to the appropriate destined treasure revealer in the future, when the middle age of a human life is fifty years. Many lifetimes later, Princess Pemasal was reborn as Longchenpa, and it was Longchenpa who revealed the transmissions of the Khandro Nyingthig.[12]

In her next life Princess Pemasal was born in Lower Drak in Central Tibet as the awareness woman known as Sangyé Kyi. When her former predilections resurfaced, she took lay ordination. The great treasure finder Nyang Nyima Özer[13] took her as his secret consort in spiritual practice. As her realization blossomed, she came to achieve the same level of enlightened view as the tertön lord himself.

Her next pure rebirth was as Jomo Pema Dröl. She was born in the Monkey Year at Kyidrong, in a place called Chorateng Lama in the northeast of Layak as the daughter of Tsurpa Sangyé. She later became the secret karma mudra consort of the great tertön Guru Chökyi Wangchuk.[14]

Jomo Pema Dröl was responsible for the construction of the Samdrup Dewachenpo temple of Layak and its contents. Later she bore a son, whom she named Pema Wangchen, and a daughter named Sangyé Kündröl. Accomplishing pure realization of dharmata, she served and benefited the Dharma and sentient beings in a great and good way.

Her next incarnation took birth in male form as the great mantra master Ngakchang Rinchen Drakpa. Born into a lineage of mantrikas in Trongsa in Yoru, Ngakchang Rinchen Drakpa later became a student of Orgyen Lingpa[15] of Yarje. He practiced *Iron Hair Hayagriva* and The Great Perfection: Padma Innermost Essence.[16] Meeting the yidam deity face to face seven times, he achieved the level of "warmth capacity" and became a great mighty one with magical powers.

His next rebirth was as a great tertön named Pema Ledrel Tsal, also known as Pangangpa Rinchen Tsuldor.[17] He was born in the Female Iron Hare Year, the son of a couple who were venerable lay tantric adepts from the Nyang clan, in a place called Rizhing, near the cliff of Koro Drak on the plateau known as Drintang in the lower region of Nyaldang Loro. His parents had to struggle hard to make ends meet, so the boy grew up in great poverty and difficulty.

One day, when no one at all would step forward to help him, he felt very heartsick and sad, and he left Koro. On the plateau of Drintang he met a middle-aged monk whom he asked, "Venerable one, where are you going?"

The monk answered, "I am not going anywhere. I have come to see you." He then drew a scroll from the folds of his robes and gave it to Pema Ledrel Tsal, commanding him, "My son, study this well. Have no doubt about the meaning of the words and take them to heart. You will have the auspicious good fortune to attain powers." With that, the monk disappeared. After a short instant of confusion, Pema Ledrel Tsal knew that he had no way of looking for him and decided to return home.

One day he read the scroll closely and found the following paragraph: "In the Female Water Ox Year, a year from now, it will be time for you to receive your share of treasure. Set forth on the tenth day of the first month of autumn. On the cliff face of Tramo Drak in Dang Valley in the region of Dakpo you will find a red swastika, an indicator of a terma. Look to the northeast of this and you will see a quart-sized cube-shaped stone. Remove the stone and you will discover the profound termas inside."

This reawakened his previous propensities, and so, inspired by this prophecy of Guru Rinpoché, Pema Ledrel Tsal went to Dang Valley. There he spent three days in a cave at Tramo Drak Cliff extracting the great termas from their place of hiding.[18] Among the treasures he uncovered was the profound teaching of the Khandro Nyingthig, which is like a wish-fulfilling gem through which one can attain the state of buddhahood in one life, the pinnacle experience of the enlightened intent of the Great Orgyen, Padmasambhava. He also discovered *The Wheel of the Union of Lamas*; *Vajrapani*

Suppressing All Fierce Ones; *Three Gods of Hayagriva Practice*; and *Sealing the Mouth of Yama*.

In Lumo Takdongmai Towa he discovered *The Poisonous Blade of Wild Planet (Rahula)*, and from the cliff of Sepularé, *The Maroon-Faced Planet (Rahula)* and *Red-Eyed Butcher*. From the cliffs of Ashu in the Den country he found the cycle of Wrathful Singhamukha and Kilaya as well as many other profound treasures, such as *Mighty Wind Lasso, The Great Capability*, and others. He became known as "the great lord of the eastern treasures."

He then embarked on his journey home and got as far as Upper Nyal. Pausing from his journey at Shotserma Valley, he spent the night with a lay tantric practitioner couple. They hosted him well, serving him with food and chang,[19] and they enjoyed much of the evening together in pleasant conversation.

The tantrika husband asked him, "Where did you come from yesterday? Why did you go there?"

Pema Ledrel Tsal replied, "Because of a prophecy I once received, I went to the Dakpo area."

The tantrika asked, "Well, did you find any termas?"

"I did," he replied.

"What were they?"

Pema Ledrel Tsal replied "The Khandro Nyingthig, pith instructions concerning three adjunct deity practices, and the cycle for accomplishing the practice of the great planet demon Rahula, as well as tantras."

"Since that is so, we supplicate you to please give us an empowerment with the casket of texts." So Pema Ledrel Tsal picked up the casket in which the texts were found and blessed the tantrika and his wife, as well as their son, Gyalsé Legpa Gyaltsen. The next morning, as he was preparing to set off, the son came to offer prostrations to him with great faith and devotion. Pema Ledrel Tsal took the youth under his wing, granting him all of the spiritual transmissions and empowerments of the secret Nyingthig teachings.

He returned home to Drintang where news of his journeys quickly spread among the local people. They said, "This Ledrel Tsal can't possibly carry out any of the duties of a tertön from a tantric lineage! Now he is trying to deceive us. Termas? How could this one possibly have termas?" And in this way the inhabitants spread rumors disparaging him.

Disappointed in his community, Pema Ledrel Tsal decided to become a wandering mendicant. He set off with four followers: Gyalsé Legpa Gyaltsen, Namkha Wangchuk, Rinchen Dorjé, and Palgyi Sengé. Passing through the areas of Jar and El, they eventually arrived in Yarlung, where they spent three days at the cliff known as Sheldrak establishing a connection with the holy site. From there they traveled on to Samyé Monastery and paid reverence to the temples there. Then at Chimphu they spent seven days at the shrine of Gegong. On about the fifth day a red woman appeared in the middle of the night, saying that she was Vajravarahi. She instructed Pema Ledrel Tsal, "Do not stay here! Go to Lhasa, where there is a student with a karmic connection to you; you should meet him." And so they decided to leave Chimphu, and they all set out for Lhasa.

Upon arriving in Lhasa, they spent about five days circumambulating the city. Meanwhile, the Omniscient Karmapa, Dharma Lord Rangjung Dorjé,[20] was tenting with his entourage on Kubum Plain near Lhasa. He sent for them, saying, "Let this tertön from the southern ravines and his disciples come to see me!" So Pema Ledrel Tsal and his students went as summoned, made prostrations to the Karmapa, and made offerings, including a pill of a brahmin's flesh,[21] a bolt of silk, and a small pouch of musk.

Rangjung Dorjé then asked the five men, master and disciples, "Do you have the termas that you withdrew from hiding? If so, you must reveal them to me."

Pema Ledrel Tsal replied, "It's only been five days since the five of us came here to perform circumambulations. We have only the original yellow scrolls that I brought forth since we have not had time to make copies of the terma texts."

Rangjung Dorjé said, "E ma ho! How wonderful that you retrieved these yellow scrolls! Please show them to me!" They gave him the scrolls for examination; he looked them over carefully, touched them to the crown of his head, and handed them back.

The group then returned to Lhasa and spent the night at the foot of an obelisk. That night, a red woman[22] wearing bone ornaments appeared in Rangjung Dorjé's dreams. She told him, "Ask for the profound pith instructions of the secret mantra approach from Pema Ledrel Tsal, who is a heart son of Orgyen Padmasambhava. Offer him some of your hair. If you do this, the teachings will flourish in the future."

The next morning, as Pema Ledrel Tsal and his group were preparing to have breakfast, an emissary sent by Rangjung Dorjé arrived and told them, "You have been summoned by the holy presence, the Gyalwa Karmapa." And so they returned with the emissary to the Karmapa's encampment for an audience. The Lord Rangjung Dorjé greeted them warmly and had his

THE THIRD KARMAPA, RANGJUNG DORJÉ

attendants serve everyone hot buttered tea and tsampa. After a time he looked at Pema Ledrel Tsal and said, "You *must* give me the oral transmission for the scrolls you had yesterday."

Pema Ledrel Tsal replied, "I could never presume to give transmission to such a high personage as you."

"But you must!" the Karmapa insisted, and bowed to Pema Ledrel Tsal with respect. Unable to refuse his request, Pema Ledrel Tsal bestowed upon him the profound treasures, the complete oral transmissions for the Khandro Nyingthig, directly from the terma writings on the yellow scrolls. Pema Ledrel Tsal thus became a guru to Karmapa Rangjung Dorjé, who then offered the group the hair of his head as a gesture of deepest respect and gratitude, saying, "Divide these clippings equally among you."

Pema Ledrel Tsal then went back to Koro Drak Cliff in the Drin Plateau region and did accomplishment meditation practice for seven months. He actually met the Guru and his consort, who granted their blessings by bestowing upon him the realization of the lineage of enlightened intent. During that time he passed on to Gyalsé Legpa Gyaltsen all of the oral transmission blessings for his spiritual lineages.

Pema Ledrel Tsal then went on to a place in front of Chöten Drak Cliff and spent three months in meditation, while Gyalsé Legpa Gyaltsen camped below. When the tertön Rinchen Lingpa[23] came to see Pema Ledrel Tsal, Gyalsé Legpa Gyaltsen responded, "Since the precious tertön is currently in retreat, there is not a chance of having an audience with him."

"In that case," Rinchen Lingpa replied, "you must bestow upon me all of the oral transmissions you have received from him." So Gyalsé Legpa Gyaltsen gave the entire body of oral transmissions for the Khandro Nyingthig to Rinchen Lingpa.

Upon finishing his retreat at Chöten Drak, Tulku Ledrel Tsal traveled to Lower Nyal. Gyalsé Legpa Gyaltsen and Rinchen Lingpa both followed after him to seek an audience and finally found him near Sechen Bumpa. Pema Ledrel Tsal asked, "Where are you two headed?"

"We have come to meet with you, Dharma Lord," they replied.

"Well, then, come on with me. I'm going to Drin Plateau." So together they set off toward the plateau. On the way, they stayed at Chöling Monastery, where Pema Ledrel Tsal gave Rinchen Lingpa the key to termas concealed within a black boulder shaped like a tortoise on a mountain pass on the route to China.[24] He said, "My son, take this key and reveal the termas hidden in that boulder. Use them to ensure benefit for beings."

Having carried out compassionate activities for the sake of beings, Pema Ledrel Tsal spent the rest of his life practicing the Khandro Nyingthig, and so found little opportunity to spread these teachings, transmitting them to only a few. He was unable to meet his destined consort as prophesied by Guru Rinpoché because he mistook an obstacle-inflicting witch for an authentic dakini. Due to outer conditions imposed by this and other circumstances, his life was cut short.

Before passing away at the age of twenty-nine, he entrusted his ward Gyalsé Legpa Gyaltsen with the yellow scrolls, saying to him and two others, "Soon I shall pass away, and some eight or ten years afterward I will return and become your student. Keep my terma teachings undamaged. I will take birth in Upper Dra of Central Tibet as the son of a father called Tenpa and a mother named Sönam. Until that time practice these teachings and take care of them, and then return them to me. Through the practice of all these teachings, the benefit of sentient beings will be accomplished. I will see you all then."

After he gave this advice, the display of his emanated form body then dissolved back into the primordial being of inner basic space, the vast expanse of reality.[25]

Pema Ledrel Tsal thus died fairly young, and not many years later, as predicted, he was reborn as the Omniscient Longchen Rabjam Drimé Özer.

Namdru Remati (Palden Lhamo)

2. His Birth and Early Life

In the experience of yogins who do not perceive things dualistically,
the fact that things manifest without truly existing is so amazing
they burst into laughter.
—Longchenpa[*]

The Omniscient King of the Dharma, Longchen Rabjam, appeared in Tibet, the Land of Snows, as the second conqueror,[1] the all-knowing lord of speech, master of the three categories of the Dzogchen teachings.[2] He was born in a village called Todrong[3] in Upper Dra Valley in Yoru, the eastern part of Central Tibet.

His father, the vajra master Tenpa Sung, was an adept master and tantric yogi, continuing the family yogic tradition as the twenty-fifth generation of the Rok clan, hailing from the noble line of Öki Kyinkorchen and Gyalwa Chokyang[4] of Ngenlam.

His paternal grandfather, the vajra master Lhasung, lived for 150 years[5] due to his accomplished practice of the healing deity Dutsimen and his achievement of the alchemical transformation of deathless nectar.

Longchenpa's mother was Dromza Sönam Gyen of the Drom clan, descended from the family of Dromtönpa Gyelwé Jungné.[6]

Shortly after her son was conceived, Sönam Gyen had a powerful dream wherein a white snow lion, with the sun and moon rising together at the point between his eyebrows and forming a swirling mass of light, entered her womb.

Later, before he was born, the primordial wisdom dakini, Namdru Remati, appeared to her in the form of a black woman with bared fangs and frowning brow, wielding a sword, and she told the mother, "A being is going

[*] Translated by Richard Barron in *The Precious Treasury of the Basic Space of Phenomena*, p. 59.

to be born to you who will be the upholder of the teachings of the dakinis." And then she disappeared. Sönam Gyen didn't know whether this being that had appeared to her had been a human or a god, but it was definitely a true appearance that she experienced.

Many other miraculous signs manifested during her pregnancy, and her son was born on Saturday, March 2, 1308, the tenth day of the second month of the lunar calendar in the Male Earth Monkey Year, in the lunar mansion of Gyalwa. His parents named their newborn son Dorjé Gyaltsen.

The moment he was born, Remati appeared again to the mother as a black woman with a sword. Taking the baby boy in her lap, she said, "I shall protect him!" Then, returning him to his mother, she vanished.

One day, after Longchenpa's birth, his mother, Sönam Gyen, was out weeding in the garden, when she was caught in a sudden downpour. In her confusion, she ran back to her house, but she forgot to bring her child, the infant Longchenpa. Once inside, she immediately remembered her son, and went back to fetch him.

To her shock, the boy was nowhere to be found, although she looked everywhere, in the midst of the pouring rain. Unable to locate him, she went back into her house crying. Just a little bit later, the guardian Remati appeared again, emerging from the storeroom. She was holding her sword and carrying the child. She scolded the mother, and almost struck Sönam Gyen with her sword, saying, "You don't care about this child who is the upholder of the dakini's heart essence teachings?" She returned the child to his mother and then vanished.

In this way the dakinis protected and upheld Longchenpa as a child, and even while he was in the womb. Throughout Dorjé Gyaltsen's childhood the goddess Namdru Remati manifested in this distinct form and watched over him.

As soon as he could speak Dorjé Gyaltsen would describe things with amazing clarity, as though recalling previous lifetimes. When he was still quite young his family moved to a place close to Khamsum Metokdrol in the area of Samyé Monastery. Blessed as he was with very powerful faith, compassion, and intelligence, by the age of five Dorjé Gyaltsen knew how to read and write as soon as the texts were shown to him, without any study at all.

At the age of seven, Dorjé Gyaltsen began studying with his father, receiving the empowerments, explanatory commentaries, pith instructions, and traditional practice methods for the Eight Commands cycle entitled The

Gathering of Sugatas, and cycles focusing on Hayagriva, Vajrakila, and The Peaceful and Wrathful Forms of Guru Rinpoché. In addition, his father, Lopön Tenpa Sung, trained him in medicine, astrology, and other fields of learning.

At Tsongdu in Drachi Valley, when he was nine, he memorized and understood the meaning of all the words in the sutras the *Prajnaparamita in Twenty-five Thousand Lines* and the *Prajnaparamita in Eight Thousand Lines* by reciting these texts aloud one hundred times each.

It was at this time that his mother, Dromza Sönam Gyen, died. Just three years later, when Longchenpa had reached the age of twelve,[7] his father, Tenpa Sung, died. And so, at such a young age, Dorjé Gyaltsen lost both his kind mother and his beloved father, who was also his first teacher. Now an orphan, the young Dorjé Gyaltsen went to the great monastery at nearby Samyé and requested ordination as a novice monk, which he received from the abbot, Samdrup Rinchen, and the preceptor, Kunga Özer. He was given the name Tsultrim Lodrö.[8]

The novice monk Tsultrim Lodrö undertook a comprehensive study of the Vinaya, the Buddha's teaching of ethics, vows, and rules for the monastic community and laypeople. By the time he was fourteen he had gained complete mastery of the subject, was able to teach its meaning to others, and even wrote his own original commentary on the Vinaya. In this way he received early recognition as a prodigy and learned scholar.

3. HIS EARLY TEACHERS AND TRAINING

Although sensory appearances do not exist, they manifest in all their variety.
Although emptiness does not exist, it extends infinitely,
reaching everywhere.
—LONGCHENPA*

WHEN HE WAS sixteen years old Tsultrim Lodrö had a vision of the dakini Sarasvati (Yangchenma). She told him that he would come to know everything naturally and spontaneously, without training or study. Yet still he went everywhere to study; he studied both Nyingma and Sarma; he trained in all the different schools and lineages without sectarian bias, and studied with many different teachers, learning as much as he possibly could.

At sixteen years of age Tsultrim Lodrö studied with the teacher Rinchen Tashi, receiving from him the empowerments and instructions of the two traditions of the Lamdré[1] cycle, two traditions of the Six Yogas of Naropa, the Six Yogas of Vajravarahi, Ghantapada's lineage of the deity Chakrasamvara, and Mahachakra Vajrapani.

With the teachers Wangchuk Yeshé, Töntsül, and Tropupa he studied the *Kalachakra Tantra* and most of the other tantric cycles of the Sarma schools, including those of the three lower tantras of kriyatantra, charyatantra, and yogatantra; and also *The Ocean of Dakas*. The teacher Lopön Töntsül taught him the process of refining mercury according to the methods of the sage Zhungkyé.

From the teacher Lopön Wanggyé he received detailed teachings on meditation deities, as well as many sadhanas and pith instructions on the tantra *The Buddha Skull Cup*, the tantra *The Dakini Pavilion*, the tradition

---

* Translated by Richard Barron in *The Precious Treasury of the Basic Space of Phenomena*, p. 59.

of Ra Lotsawa for the deity Vajrabhairava, the cycle concerning subtle
energy for the deity Dzambhala, the deity Kurukulle, the six consorts of
the sages, *Maitreya*, the sixteen arhats, Bhaishajyaguru,[2] and so forth. From
the precious master Tropupa he received *The Vajra Garland* and the cycles
of the protective deity of the tantra *The Vajra Pavilion*.

From Zaplunga Rinpoché he received the teaching cycles of the Tsalpa
School; Gotsangpa's teachings on the path; Pacification according to the
Early, Middle, and Later Traditions of the Shijé School of Padampa Sangyé;[3]
and the teachings of the Chöd School of Machig Labdrön.

At nineteen Tsultrim Lodrö went to the famous Sangphu Neutok school[4]
in the Sangphu uplands, where he studied principally with the great teacher
Tsengönpa,[5] the administrator Chöpal Gyaltsen,[6] and Zhönnu Rinchen,
who was renowned as a second Dharmakirti. With these three masters he
studied the Five Treatises of Maitreya, treatises on logic by Dignaga and
Dharmakirti such as the *Compendium of Valid Cognition*, the *Detailed Commentary on the Compendium of Valid Cognition*, as well as all of the main
texts and commentaries concerning Prajnaparamita, and Madhyamaka
(Middle Way). Learning both the words and the underlying meaning of
these texts, he became quite erudite.

With the translator Lodrö Tenpa of Pang he studied Sanskrit, poetry,
grammar, composition, drama, and many inner treatises such as the Five
Profound Sutras, which include the *Sutra of the King of Contemplation*,[7] and
the *Detailed Commentary on the Heart of Perfect Wisdom* (*Prajnaparami-
tahridaya*) texts. In this way he reached the pinnacle of knowledge.

With the teacher Zhönnu Gyalpo he studied the complete tradition of
the great Nagarjuna, such as Nagarjuna's Six Collections of Reasoning—
Collected Aphorisms (a commentary on the Four Noble Truths), *Source
Verses on Sublime Knowing*, *Sixty Verses on Reasoning*, *Seventy Verses on
Emptiness*, *Minute Scrutiny*, and *Refutation of Arguments*—as well as his
Commentary on the Definitive Collection of the Ultimate and *Praise of the
Basic Space of Phenomena*. He also studied the *Clearly Worded Commentary*
and *Introduction to Madhyamaka*, both by Chandrakirti.

With Loten Panglo Chenpo he studied detailed explanations of the
Seven Treatises on Valid Cognition and explanations of the class of profound sutras such as the *Sutra of the King of Contemplation*, as well as all of
the sources for the fields of secular knowledge, like the source text *The Mirror of Poetics* and the commentary on it. Studying these in their entirety, he
came to master thoroughly all of the words and their underlying meaning
in three years.

He then wandered to different places and *shedras*, centers where scriptures and correct reasoning were taught, and studied with many famous scholars. He encountered no obstacles in mastering the full range of root texts, and developed the dynamic energy of his wisdom. He independently achieved the great accomplishment of unobstructed intelligence. He received all the teachings and transmissions of both the old and new tantras of the various lineages that were taught in Tibet at that time. His fame as a supreme scholar resounded like a great drum in all directions; his degree of learning was undisputed and unparalleled, and he was conferred the title "Longchen Rabjampa" (Infinitely Great Learned One Who Is Like the Vast Expanse of Space).[8] Henceforth he was known by this title.[9] He also became known as "Samyé Lungmangpa" (Samyé's Recipient of Many Transmissions).

While studying at Sangphu the young Longchenpa practiced the stages of approach and accomplishment for deities associated with the development of sublime knowing, such as Manjugosha, Achala, Tara, Sarasvati, and White Vajravarahi, and was blessed with visions of them all. In particular, the goddess Sarasvati took him by the hand and spent seven days showing him the four continents and Mt. Sumeru so that he developed the force of his unparalleled intellect. He also received a prophecy of his imminent enlightenment from her. In *Playful Delight of Youthfulness*, his prayer of praise to Sarasvati, he writes:

> Ah! Goddess of good fortune,
> my longtime aspiration has been realized today!

From that time on he was never separate from Sarasvati, who manifested in various different forms for him. As he said:

> Your embodiments, in a mass of light,
> are white, yellow, red, and green.
> Sometimes, within canopies of clouds,
> your form is multicolored—brilliant white, crimson, dark blue.
> You appear in forms that play or move or stand.

In addition, with Zhönnu Döndrup of Denbak, Ten Phakpa, and Nyotingmawa Sangyé Drakpa, he studied the Collected Tantras of the Nyingma School, the *Discourse on United Intent*, *The Web of Magical Display*, and the mind teachings, and received many initiations and pith instructions on other important Nyingma tantras, such as the *Do* (sutras) of Anuyoga, the *Mayajalatantra* of Mahayoga, and the Semdé (Mind) class teachings of Atiyoga.

With Zhönnu Dorjé he studied Shantideva's *Guide to the Bodhisattva's Way of Life* and *A Compendium of Lessons*, as well as the Cycle of Yidams of Atisha from the Kadampa lineage. He also studied the *Kalachakra Six-Limbed Yoga* and the Six Yogas of Naropa.

Under his preceptor[10] he studied the Cycle of Tropupa and the Dharma Cycle of Kharak, as well as the Ocean of Means of Attainment, One Hundred Brief Doctrines, Transmissions of the Vinaya, and a great many others.

From several khenpos he received teachings on the Ocean of Sadhanas, the Ocean of Dakinis, One Hundred Religious Histories, the *Scriptural Transmission of the Vinaya*, the extensive, middle-length, and abridged classes of sutras, the *Vajra Cutter Sutra*, the *Condensed Verses on the Perfection of Sublime Knowing*, the *Heart of Sublime Knowing*, the *Prajnaparamitasutra in Ten Thousand Lines*, the *Methods in One Hundred and Fifty Verses*, and other texts.

With the Lord of the Dharma Karmapa Rangjung Dorjé Longchenpa studied such teachings as the *Six Techniques of Union* from the Kalachakra cycle, including the auxiliary methods for dispelling hindrances; the Six Yogas of Naropa; the *Direct Introduction to the Three Kayas*; "The Tradition of the King" for the form of the supremely compassionate Avalokiteshvara called Jinasagara; and the tantras of Guhyasamaja, Samputa, Mahamaya, and the red and black forms of Yamantaka.[11]

Under Lopön Wangtsul he studied *The Six-Limbed Yoga*, the *Oddiyana Tradition of Ritual Service*, teachings of vital energy (*lung kor*), and many other teachings as well.

With Zhöndor of Shuksep[12] he studied Saraha's three Doha Cycles, the Three Cycles of Spiritual Teachings for Mountain Retreat, the *One Hundred Points of Interdependent Connection*, and other works.

Lama Jamyangpa imparted to him the full range of instructions concerning the astrological charts of the *Kalachakra Tantra*, as well as the *Two Chapters*, the tantra *The Vajra Pinnacle*, the *Source Tantra of Manjushri*, *The Vajra Source*, the *Compendium of Suchness*, the tantra *Compendium of Suchness for Refining Lower Realms*, the tantra *Immutable Basic Space*, the tantra *All-Knowing One*, and *The Clear Meaning of Consecration*.

With the great Sakya master Lama Dampa Sönam Gyaltsen[13] Longchenpa studied the *Great Awakening of Motivation* as well as all of the instructions of *The Three Continua*. With Lama Tsongdupa he studied the

Eight Commands cycle of Guru Chöwang entitled *The Complete Secret*; the Condensed Quintessence Cycle of Mahakarunika; the Dzogchen cycle *Union of All Buddhas in Equalness*; the practice of Khorwa Dongtruk; *The Guru*; the *Gathering of Secrets*; the practice of the protective deity Maning Nakpo;[14] and such secular texts as the *Hundred Teachings on Extracting the Vital Essence, The Patra* (a technical manual for defensive measures against invasion), *The Catapult of Fire and Water*, and *The Means of Ensuring Great Power.*

From Kangmarwa he received teachings on the protective deities Tsedak Palapatra, Tsatsa Nyonpa, Tsitta Marpo, the wrathful *mamo* goddess Dugi Pudri, and Duwa Lungzhon;[15] *The Black Stupa* (concerning seven non-Buddhist deities); and the pith instructions for preventing or bringing down hailstorms. Tingma Sangyé Drako transmitted to him such teachings as The Gathering of Sugatas (a cycle focusing on the Eight Commands that was a terma teaching of Nyang), Namchak Umro, Vajrakilaya, the dakini Guhyajnana, the protective deity Lekden, and the guardian deities Takshön and Sengshön.

He mastered the empowerments and oral transmission blessings of both the Nyingma and Sarma Schools of secret mantra, explanations of many major and minor source texts of the sutra and tantra traditions, explanatory commentaries and profound teachings, as well as all major secular subjects as grammar, poetics, and astrology. Thus, Longchenpa completed his study and training in the entire range of fields of inquiry.

4. Leaving Sangphu and Dark Retreat

Below rocky cliffs,
a vivid sense of impermanence and disenchantment dawns,
clear and inspired, helping us to achieve
the union of calm abiding and penetrating insight.
—Longchenpa*

WHILE STILL at Sangphu, in general he felt boundless sorrow and disillusionment with the condition of the world of samsara, and the urge to live in solitude dawned in him. In particular, Longchenpa began to feel distaste for the rough and discourteous nature of some of the monks from the Kham province of eastern Tibet that were living at Sangphu. Jealous of his accomplishment, they passed up no opportunity to make his life difficult, and actually threw him out of his rooms seven times!

Longchenpa wrote many tracts on the faults of these eastern Tibetans, which he then carried to the teaching throne in his dormitory, but to no avail; the Khampas' belligerent behavior toward him and others continued unabated. Finally, he decided that it was time to leave Sangphu for good, and to find an auspicious place of solitude to practice without distraction what he had so diligently studied.

His preceptor, as well as his fellow students, who perceived the rare genius qualities of this young holy man, could not bear the idea of his departure, and with heartfelt sorrow and sincere pleas tried to talk him out of the idea. But Longchenpa's mind was made up, and he prepared to set out from Sangphu.

As he was finally departing in the early morning, he encountered a monk friend in front of the hall housing the statues known as Lotsawai Kubum.[1]

---

* Translated by Adam Pearcey in *Mind in Comfort and Ease*, p. 229.

"Where are you going?" his friend asked.

"Since there is no place for me to stay among those Khampas, I am leaving here," he said.

His friend shared Longchenpa's feelings on the aggressive behavior of the Khampa monks. He offered encouragement, saying, "Now that you have officially left the college, and there is no restriction on what you can write, you should publicize the infamy of those Khampas." Longchenpa replied, "Here, I want you to have this," and gave the monk a copy of a poem he had composed about his difficulties with the Khampas entitled "Saddened by My Circumstances," a poem based on the order of the Tibetan alphabet,[2] which his friend then went and attached to the throne in the teaching court.

Later that day, when the Khampas saw it, they removed the letter from sight, but the thirty-line poem, beginning with the line "Like the ogres who roam in Kalinga . . ." eventually circulated over all the kingdom.

Wearing only the barest necessities of clothing—the skirt and vest that all Tibetan children wear in monastic schools—he shook the dust of Sangphu off his feet and traveled toward the higher elevations of Upper Uru in Central Tibet, begging along the road to sustain himself.

Resting in a meadow in Lower Cha Valley, he met a scholar named Geshé Töntsül from Gyama. Longchenpa asked him whether there was a cave associated with Druptop Chokla[3] in Gya-mé.

The scholar replied, "I know that Master Chokla stayed in an excellent cliffside cave."

Longchenpa said, "I gathered a full bag of barley while begging, so I feel I should stay there for the winter."

"Please do so! I will stay as well and serve you as your attendant," Töntsül suggested.

In the village Longchenpa performed a ritual for the stillborn child of a lay tantric practitioner. Taking the small offering that he received in exchange, he spent the next eight months in the cave of Chokla in complete, continual darkness, day and night.[4]

At dawn, between his meditation sessions, he would pass along the teachings of the six paramitas of the bodhisattva to the scholar Töntsül. Otherwise, he remained in meditative absorption.

After five months of practice in total darkness, one morning at dawn Longchenpa had a profound experience. He heard the sounds of melodious singing, accompanied by the music of cymbals. He found himself in a low valley, with sandy dunes and a waterfall. Above him he saw a horse, caparisoned with a leather mail saddle and small bells. Its rider was a sixteen-year-old girl of unparalleled loveliness, richly dressed in a brocade robe, a jeweled tiara, and a golden veil, with gold and turquoise ornaments. He clasped the hem of the girl's robe and supplicated her, saying, "Exalted lady,[5] take me under your compassionate care!"

She removed her crown of precious gems from her head and placed it on his head, saying, "From now on I shall always bless you and grant you siddhis." She also prophesied that he would meet his destined guru, the great Rigdzin Kumaradza.

Although he awakened at sunrise for the next three days, he remained absorbed in a state of bliss, clarity, and nonconceptual awareness. Thereafter, he spent a month deeply immersed in the same state. "I did not wake up for a long time," he said later. This was a very auspicious sign that he would soon encounter a transmission connected with the secret inner teachings of Dzogchen, the Great Perfection, the pinnacle teachings of Buddhism.

Having finished his retreat, Longchenpa performed one hundred repetitions of the ritual of Sarvavid Vairochana[6] to benefit his parents. Thinking that this would benefit him greatly, too, Töntsül requested the empowerment from Longchenpa, who agreed. Longchenpa drew the complete mandala in colored sand in a small clearing next to a spring, and gave the empowerment to Töntsül, a lay tantrika, and about thirty other men and women.[7]

RIGDZIN KUMARADZA

5. Meeting the Guru Kumaradza

You must serve, in the best possible way, a noble teacher
and purify your mind through study, reflection, and meditation.
In particular, you should spend your days and nights
diligently applying yourself to the essential instructions of the oral lineage.
—LONGCHENPA*

AT THE AGE of twenty-seven Longchenpa set out to meet his true destined guru, Rigdzin Kumaradza, in the uplands of Yartokyam. On the way he met Yakdé Panchen, who urged him to come and pay homage to the Omniscient Karmapa Rangjung Dorjé, but Longchenpa respectfully declined, focused as he was on his journey to meet his guru.

When he reached the Yartokyam uplands, he first set eyes on the awareness holder Kumaradza, who lived with his group of disciples in a traveling camp of about seventy felt windbreak tents. As soon as he saw Kumaradza, Longchenpa knew with certainty that before him was Vimalamitra in person.

The guru himself was extremely delighted, and said, "Last night I dreamed of an amazing bird. It announced itself as a divine bird, surrounded by a flock of a thousand smaller birds. The birds took my texts and flew away in all directions. When I first laid eyes on you, I immediately knew that you would become a holder of my lineage. I will give you the complete transmission."

On the evening before the teachings were finally to begin, two administrators came to him carrying a large basket, and asked, "O scholar of Samyé, where is your contribution to the cost of the teachings? They begin tomorrow, and we are taking up a collection of seven loads of barley."

* Translated by Adam Pearcey in *Mind in Comfort and Ease*, p. 232.

Longchenpa replied, "I don't even have one single measure[1] of barley, but since the guru told me I would receive the teachings from him, I have remained here."

They left, saying, "If you can't handle your share for these teachings, who will cover your contribution?"

He thought to himself, "I should not approach the guru without an offering for his teachings. Since in former lives I did not accumulate enough merit, even though I have waited with such deprivation I am now to be the only person excluded from the teachings because I do not have any material contribution. I must leave the Lama.

"I am too ashamed to head out during daylight. I will leave before dawn tomorrow morning and make sure I reach the lower end of the valley before anyone awakens."

His plan now in place, he went to sleep. He awoke before dawn. Just as he was about to leave, someone came to summon him, saying, "O scholar of Samyé, come right now! The guru would like to see you."

He thought, "I am all set to leave, but it would not be right to ignore the guru's wish," and so he went to Kumaradza. Smiling, the guru said to him, "Don't be so troubled! Sit with me and let's have some tea."

He then sent for the administrators and told them, "This scholar has already offered his tribute inwardly. I will cover his share of the contribution for the teachings, so don't press him about it. I would rather that he be present than all of the others who plan to receive my teachings."

Later Kumaradza told him, "I had a dream in which I met a scholar who I was told was Vimalamitra, wearing a scholar's cap and carrying a book. He said to me, 'This fellow Drimé Özer is a holy man who has prayed and aspired to protect and uphold my teachings. You will give him the complete oral instructions, with nothing lacking. He will become the lineage holder of your teachings and a protector of the Dzogchen doctrine.'"

To encourage detachment from worldly things in the hearts of his students, the awareness holder Kumaradza had no fixed home. That spring and summer, while Longchenpa was receiving teachings from Kumaradza, the camp moved nine times, from one deserted valley to another. Just as he got settled, the time would come to move again, giving him no opportunity to obtain food or clothing. So exhausted was Longchenpa's body from the penetrating cold and the icy terrain, and so worn his clothing, that even the young monks and watchdogs spurned him. In these and other ways he endured inconceivable hardship for the sake of the Dharma.

The next year Kumaradza and Longchenpa, teacher and student, traveled together to Shampo Glacier. There the guru gave Longchenpa many empowerments and instructions, and especially the teachings of the unsurpassable secret: the outer, inner, secret, and innermost secret cycles of the Dzogchen approach of clear light; the four volumes of profound pith instructions; and the seventeen tantras, such as the *Reverberation of Sound Tantra*, the most kingly of all tantras, together with the 119 pith instructions.

He also conferred the practice cycles, empowerments, and oral permission blessings, secondary activity rituals, and traditional rites for Ekajati, the great guardian of conditioned existence; the lord protector Lekden and his consort; the planetary spirit Rahula; Dorjé Legpa; and all the other rites of the lineage protectors.

All this time Longchenpa had very few provisions. He sustained himself on several pounds of barley flour and about twenty-one pills of mercury. When snow fell, he would wrap himself in a sack and use it as both a bed and a robe. It was under these circumstances of great privation that he received all of Kumaradza's spiritual instructions, including the Vima Nyingthig teachings and other Nyingthig instructions, like water poured from one vessel into another. By practicing night and day, he realized the same attainment as his teacher

Finally, Kumaradza empowered Longchenpa as his Dharma heir, and as the lineage holder of the Nyingthig transmissions for future disciples. In turn, Longchenpa vowed to practice in retreat for six years. The protector deities of the lineage actually appeared and offered their sadhanas, pith instructions, and life force essence mantras to Longchenpa.

In particular, Rahula promised him that not one of his lineage holders would be harmed by poisons, and offered him his own seal as an amulet against contamination and poisoning. It was a red emblem, renowned as the "seal of the planet Rahu," and marked with designs of the ten syllables of the power mantra from the Kalachakra cycle and inscribed with Rahula's own name. It could make a clear impression through hundreds of sheets of paper all at the same time. Rahula also promised to serve Longchenpa in whatever ways he was commanded.

Over time Longchenpa performed seven ceremonies for summoning the presence of Rahula. Once, years later, while Longchenpa was staying in Bhutan, the goat that had been selected as the symbolic representation of Rahula's spirit during the ceremony got stuck in a thorn thicket somewhere nearby, where it died and could not be extracted.

Za Rahula

The Omniscient One commanded the wild planetary guardian, "Bring the killer of this goat here quickly!" A great dust storm swept up, uprooting the whole thicket and carrying the thorny bushes to near Longchenpa's dwelling. This and many other such incidents that happened were witnessed by all who were there.

Machig Labdrön

6. Visions and Retreats

As a beginner, it is most important that you secure your own well-being,
guarding your mind in solitude, abandoning distractions and busyness,
avoiding unfavorable situations,
and subduing the mental afflictions with appropriate antidotes.
—Longchenpa*

Then Longchenpa went alone to the Chimphu uplands, where he renewed his firm vow to Kumaradza—not to stray from his purpose in thought, word, or deed for six years. Initially, while he was staying at the ridge known as Lhündrup Gang, he beheld the form of Black Vajravarahi for seven days, and from time to time he had visions of Guru Drakpo and the twenty-one-headed form of the deity Mahottara surrounded by the 724 deities of the Eight Commands. Dorjé Yudrönma offered him her own outer, inner, and secret sadhana practices, and Dzambhala presented him with a gem.

While he stayed at Gegong he had a vision of a peaceful form of Guru Rinpoché. He also journeyed to the pure realm of Khechara, where he experienced numerous marvels. In one instance he taught the Dharma to the dakinis there. They cast flowers of auspicious blessings on him, and escorted him for a short distance when he left, offering him the permission blessings of the Nyingthig teachings. He was continually immersed in such pure visions.

At Ge-ur he had visions of bodies of light—standing forms of Red Vajravarahi, Vajrasattva, Hayagriva, Tara, and Amitayus. Then, as he practiced in a charnel ground, deities revealed their forms to him and undertook to carry out his enlightened activities.

* Translated by Adam Pearcey in *Mind in Comfort and Ease*, p. 232.

Among these were the dark-blue form of Ekajati, bearing a club and riding a wolf bitch; Rahula, the planetary mara; Dorjé Legpa, the four-armed Dharma protector; Zhanglön Dorjé Duddül; and the guardians known as the "twenty-one protectors." He discussed the Dharma with dakinis just as you or I would speak to another person.

During this period, whenever the need arose, he would immediately go to Kumaradza to clarify his understanding, then meditate one-pointedly, pleasing him to the highest degree with his offerings of Dharma practice, dynamic realization of view, progress and fortitude in meditation, and wisdom of knowing all knowable subjects. He also made the offering of all his material possessions seven times.

Longchenpa described his attainments by writing: "There is no more attachment to samsara in me. I am liberated from the chains of hope and fear. I always abide in the view and meditation of absolute Dzogpa Chenpo."[1]

At Kani Gozhi the timeless awareness embodiment of Machig Lapkyi Drönma took him under her care, giving him the transmission of her teachings on Chöd.

7. Turning the Dharma Wheel

The welfare of others cannot be accomplished
without the higher faculties of perception,
so strive diligently for your own well-being
while mentally considering the welfare of others.
—LONGCHENPA*

AT THIRTY-ONE, while still in retreat, Longchenpa for the first time
conferred the empowerment and instructions of the Vima Nyingthig
upon his fortunate disciples at Shuksep in the Nyipu uplands near White
Skull Snow Mountain. For some time after, all the surroundings turned to
pure lights, mystical sounds, and divine appearances.

Soon after, his yogi disciple Özer Gocha found the text of Khandro
Nyingthig, discovered as a terma by Longchenpa's previous incarnation,
Pema Ledrel Tsal. He brought it to Longchenpa and made his guru an offer-
ing of the text.

The Dharma protectress Shenpa Sogdrubma[1] also presented Longchenpa
with a copy of the same text. At the time he was speaking with one Lama
Remawa when a black woman approached, placed a volume in his hands,
and vanished without a trace. Lama Remawa saw that the volume was a text
entitled the Khandro Nyingthig. Amazed, he brought this to Longchenpa's
attention.

Knowing that the visitation had been an exhortation by the goddess Sogdrubma, the master Longchen Rabjam made a commitment to teach the
Khandro Nyingthig at the Chimphu uplands.

Although he was the reincarnation of Pema Ledrel Tsal, the tertön who
discovered the terma teachings, in order to show the importance of pre-

---

* Translated by Adam Pearcey in *Mind in Comfort and Ease*, p. 233.

serving the transmission lineage for future followers Longchenpa sought out Gyalsé Legpa Gyaltsen, Pema Ledrel Tsal's Dharma heir, to request teachings, and the two of them began to talk and share information. It soon became obvious to Gyalsé Legpa Gyaltsen that this was indeed his root guru, Pema Ledrel Tsal, returned within a new body, and that all of the qualities that he had perceived in his guru were present in Longchenpa. Just like someone moving from one building to another, his consciousness had moved from one body into another one.

He said to Longchenpa, "Truly, you are my root guru, and I need to offer these teachings back to you. Here are the texts you left with me." With that, he reverently handed the texts back to Longchenpa.

But Longchenpa said, "That won't do! It isn't that I am denying that I was your root guru in my previous life. But because my form had changed, it is vital for the integrity of the lineage that I receive the teachings from you now in a formal transmission."

So, even though Gyalsé Legpa Gyaltsen did not feel worthy of offering them to his master, because of the need to uphold the transmission lineage he bestowed the entire body of teachings of the Khandro Nyingthig cycle on Longchenpa. This is how Longchenpa received the authentic and pure unbroken lineage of the terma transmission of the Khandro Nyingthig.

During the middle month of autumn of the Hare Year, when he was thirty-two, he again taught the Vima Nyingthig cycle to eight fortunate men and women, including yogi Özer Gocha, at Rimochen in the Chimphu uplands near Samyé.

At some point during the empowerment the glorious guardian goddess of mantra, Ekajati, took possession of a yogini. When the other students expressed doubts about the authenticity of what had taken place, Longchenpa replied, "No need to worry. This woman has truly been possessed by a dakini. As I am a yogi who has realized that mind and the sensory appearances it perceives are of one taste, no obstacles will come of it."

Thereupon the yogini prostrated to her guru and, looking toward the mandala, said, "Why is there no peacock feather?" Longchenpa replied, "I have visualized it in my mind." She retorted, "How could such a spiritual symbol simply be imagined?"

She then removed the tripods supporting the vase's platform, set three vases on the shrine, and placed these vases fastened together in a row. Longchenpa then proceeded to perform the ritual in perfect detail, whereupon the yogini folded her hands and exclaimed, "This is wonderful!"

MAMO EKAJATI

However, when he pronounced the word *rigs* as *rig*, dropping the final letter, she cried out, "No, no! It's pronounced *rigs*!"[2] And when Longchenpa recited the mantra, the yogini said to him, "Imitate my way of doing it!" Then, in the language of the dakinis, she chanted the mantra slowly to a haunting melody, captivating the hearts of all who heard her.

During the main part of the empowerment she sang a song about the view and meditation that are free of conceptual speculation:

Though the mind that is free of meditation may be enjoyable,
Oh, how happy is the meditation that is free of the mind!

She exclaimed, "These meager offerings will never do!" and offered a sweet and melodious song instead. During the ganachakra, when the consecrated alcohol nectar was served to the guru, the yogini said, "This is the samaya substance of the dakinis, so by all means partake." And she served it to him and told him to drink it all until there was none left.[3]

Inspired, the gathered students danced and sang with joy, experiencing a one-pointed and utterly lucid state of mind. In this state, they actually saw the ephemeral forms of dakas, dakinis, and Dharma protectors.

A black woman appeared and said, "The first portion of the flour you offered is stale," while the oath-bound protector Dorjé Legpa took the form of a white man who said, "You neglected to put an ornament of red meat on my torma offering."

The protector Tsomo Dangla came as a white man riding on a white horse, seeking a torma offering, but refused the red torma of meat that was offered to him. Hosts of dakas and dakinis raised a ceremonial parasol over Longchenpa's head and circumambulated him; they shouted wrathful syllables like HUM and PHAT, making a terrific uproar. Many other such inconceivable miraculous events took place that night.

One of the yogis present was terrified and said, "Tonight heaven and earth have changed places! No doubt these beings are bent on having our flesh and blood!"

Likewise, other protective deities such as Odé Küngyal,[4] Nyenchen Tanglha,[5] and the seven Menmo sisters[6] came to receive their torma offerings.

Then Vajravarahi herself actually appeared to them, her form blue-black and ornamented with jewels and bones. She conversed with Longchenpa, saying, "Tonight is a wild night of great significance. I have come to spy on your worthy students. How is your holy guru's health?" Longchenpa replied, "This year his health has almost failed. Now what will happen?"

The dakini replied, "How could an emanation of a buddha experience obstacles? The obstacles are the expression of his intention on behalf of his disciples. Don't you realize that he is Vimalamitra returned to Tibet?"

"How long will he live?" asked Longchenpa.

"He will live at least until the next Year of the Sheep. After that, whether he lives longer or not will depend on the worthiness and merit of his disciples."

"But haven't I been urged by my guru Kumaradza to help others?"

"Indeed, yes!"

"If I practice intensively in solitude, will I attain the body of light? Or, if

I work to serve others instead, of how much benefit will that be? And how long can I live?"

She replied, "Even if you attain the body of light, you must help other sentient beings. Definitely serve others, and you will live for another thirty years."

Longchenpa asked, "Which are the guardian deities of my teachings?"

"There are so many. All of your guru's guardians are also yours. In particular, your guardian is Dorjé Yudrönma, so your ability to help others is associated with her direction, the southwest. There your ability to help others in a future lifetime will be even greater than it is now."[7]

Longchenpa pressed her further: "Well, is that due to my teaching of the Khandro Nyingthig? Is it all right for me to confer its empowerment and instructions?"

"Yes, of course! No fault in that, no fault at all. You are without question the holder of these teachings."

"So people won't think me a charlatan or hypocrite?" he asked.

"What's the point of paying attention to slander and gossip? I myself will gather the worthy recipients to assemble and meet you. Anyway, those who are unfortunate would slander even the Buddha."

Longchenpa asked, "Should I confer the Nyingthig teachings only at sites holy to Dorjé Yudrönma?"

She replied, "Since dakas and dakinis gather here naturally, you should confer them here." She also prophesied clearly that there were terma caches hidden at Bumthang in Bhutan.

Knowing the preciousness of this opportunity, Longchenpa pursued with more questions, asking, "Will I meet the great master Padmasambhava?"

"You will meet him where three upland regions converge and the slopes of three mountains meet, on the right side of a small cliff cave facing west."

"And will I meet Vimalamitra?"

She retorted, "You have already met him!" [8]

"This view that I have realized, is it the ultimate intent underlying the Nyingthig teachings?"

"There can be no error or confusion with respect to the ultimate," she responded.

A master named Rinchen Dorjé, who was also present at the time, asked her, "Where is Pangangpa Rinchen Dorjé?"[9]

Pointing her finger at the guru Longchenpa, she said, "Here he is!"

But the guru Longchenpa protested, "He was to be reborn in Bumthang in his next lifetime, so how can I be he?"

"That is so, but he was not born there, as it happens, for it became necessary for him to explore some sambhogakaya pure realms. After having discovered and revealed his terma treasures, the master Pangangpa Rinchen Dorjé was to practice in secrecy for several years.

"Had he done so, he would have mastered the training on the sambhogakaya level and experienced the inner radiance of being for his own benefit, and he would have been of great service to others.

"But he did not preserve this secrecy, and so did not live out his full life span. Now he has been reborn as you, and these visions of clear light and inner radiance that you have experienced in your spiritual practice are the result of his brief exploration of those sambhogakaya realms."

Longchenpa continued, "Will I achieve the rainbow body, wherein my body will vanish without a trace upon my death?"

The dakini answered, "You could achieve that right now if you were to meditate in solitude, but if you serve others, you will be liberated in the bardo. Your emanation will take rebirth in Bumthang and will serve others.[10] He will also journey to the land of Oddiyana and there manifest as one who awakens to buddhahood."

He persisted, "Which cycle of the Nyingthig teachings will allow me to be of the most benefit, that of Vimalamitra or that of the Dakini?"

"Both will be of benefit," she said. "The teachings of Vimalamitra will last for one hundred years, those of the dakini for five hundred years, beginning now."

Longchenpa felt greatly inspired, and rose from his seat, singing a vajra song that ended with the following lines:

> This life is bliss and my next lifetime will be happy.
> What bliss there will be in recognizing the true nature of the bardo.
> Now I shall go from bliss to even greater bliss.
> I make this song my offering, O Three Jewels.
> Please rejoice, you hosts of dakas and dakinis!

Everyone present saw incredible hosts of dakinis, all of whom dissolved into the guru. Then they witnessed still other marvels, such as the guru transforming himself into the forms of sambhogakaya deities for some time. A rain of flowers fell, and rainbows, beams, and circles of multicolored lights were seen all over the mountain. All the disciples at the gathering were dancing and singing, filled with ecstatic wisdom energy. For a long time, a month or so, the minds of the yogi disciples merged into a deep clear-light awareness, transcending distinctions of sleeping or waking.

On the twenty-eighth day of that same month, the great master Padmasambhava came from the southwest frontier, his complexion white and radiant, wearing a silk brocade cloak and a cap of soft antelope skin, and surrounded by an enormous retinue. Onlookers saw him dissolve into the guru Longchenpa. That night dakinis wearing bone ornaments approached, flying to and fro in the sky, and honored him by making offerings to the guru. Three dark brown women danced and sang:

> We have come, we have come,
> We have come from the realm of supreme bliss.
> We have come to spy on your worthy disciples.
> We have come to check on the purity of their samaya.
> O child of spiritual heritage,
> Please help beings!

Then, when Longchenpa was performing the inner offering part of the ceremony, the great master Padmasambhava appeared again. To his right was Vimalamitra, to his left was Vajravarahi, and in front of him were dakas and dakinis blowing thigh-bone trumpets. Behind him were many tantric yogis. Surrounding him were multitudes of dakinis wearing golden robes, dancing and singing. In the midst of all this, the guru Longchenpa rose from his seat and sang this vajra song:

> O yogis, how happy and joyous it is!
> Tonight, in the Unexcelled Pure Land,[11]
> In one's own body, the palace of the peaceful and wrathful deities,
> The mandala of buddhas, the union of clarity and emptiness
>   flourishes.
>
> The Buddha is not somewhere else outside,
> But within us! . . .
> This is due to the kindness of the Lama.
> The Lama is not outside,
> But within us;

The Lama of primordial purity and spontaneous presence
Dwells in the state of clarity and emptiness, free from
   apprehensions. . . .

O meditators, you who hold your minds one-pointedly,
Do not hold your mind at one place, but let it go at ease.
As the mind is emptiness, openness, whether it goes or stays.
Whatever arises is the play of wisdom.

By knowing the process of the inner five lights,
The outer lights of sun and moon have arisen continuously;
By ending inner thoughts at their foundation,
Good and bad outer circumstances have arisen as great bliss.

By increasing the inner bindus,
The clouds of outer dakinis have amassed.
By freeing the inner knots of the light channels,
The outer knots of perceiver and perceived are freed.

I go to the state of clarity and great bliss.
O vajra brothers and sisters, how happy and joyous it is!

At that point the white goddess Dorjé Yudrönma arrived with the seven sisters in her retinue, and said, "We ask that you come to our realm."

The guru Longchenpa replied, "I want to live forever in your realm," to which the goddess answered, "I would rejoice if you were to stay there always, but it seems you won't stay beyond midwinter."

He then asked, "Why have you come to see me?"

The goddess responded, "Since I was bound under oath to the Guru Padmasambhava, I have followed after his terma teachings."

"But the teachings were revealed elsewhere, and the one who revealed them has passed away. What can you achieve here?"

"The teachings were revealed elsewhere but their meaning is right here. Although your former incarnation passed away, your good fortune did not die, nor have we the guardians, and so we have come."

The guardian deities then uttered prophecies, saying, "Because these teachings are so sacred, their power could present obstacles to your longevity; it would be best if you taught them sparingly."

DORJÉ YUDRÖNMA

Longchenpa asked, "Will I receive the scrolls on which these terma teachings are written into my possession?"

"Of course, of course! We are surely keeping that in mind," said Dorjé Yudrönma. "Don't you recall that I granted you siddhis in Uru?"

"I recall what happened in the cave of Chokla.[12] Was that you, Dorjé Yudrönma?"

"No, no! Then I was Vajravarahi. Didn't you recognize me? I need to take two distinct forms: a mundane one for carrying out enlightened activities and a transcendent one for conferring the most sublime siddhi."

Then Longchenpa asked, "In certain teaching cycles the explanations focus on the bindu energies. Why is the third empowerment conferred employing an actual consort?"[13]

She answered, "This method is intended to bring those with much desire to the spiritual path. For those who have renounced desire, it is sufficient for the consort to be visualized."[14]

Longchenpa asked, "When I introduce students to their true nature, do I explain that one rests in the unborn nature of thought or that one rests the mind without making any evaluation?"

She answered, "What is the point of stabilizing one's thought processes? Introduce them to the vast and open expanse that has been free and liberated from the very beginning!"

Longchenpa said, "Very well, but since there seem to be so many who are explaining these Nyingthig teachings, why should I teach? There are, for example, teachers such as Karmapa and Rinchen Lingpa who simply confer the oral transmissions to 'give people a handle' on the teachings, so to speak."

"I do not like their methods of teaching," she replied. "Even a clay cup has a handle, so how could that be enough? There have to be a few who truly take ownership and possession of that cup."

"What about the termas discovered by Rinchen Lingpa?" asked Longchenpa.

"They exist, it is true, but they are not the pure Nyingthig teachings," said Dorjé Yudrönma.

Then he asked, "Why is it that I have realized you and gained your accomplishments without meditating upon you?"

Dorjé Yudrönma replied, "Am I a deity upon whom you must meditate? Have I a mantra you must recite? Am I an object of worship? Don't you know that I am always present before all yogis who uphold their samaya and gain realization? Throughout all of your lifetimes our connection has been beyond our meeting and parting in the ordinary sense."

"The riches of the princess[15] that are concealed in Chimphu: where are they located?" Longchenpa queried.

"They can be found in a rock crag shaped like a food-offering torma with its top cut off. But the time is not yet ripe for them to be discovered."[16]

He asked her, "When will the termas of Vimalamitra be revealed?"

She replied, "Five years from now a tantric practitioner dressed in white will reveal these teachings and disseminate them. The four volumes of these profound teachings will come into your hands."[17]

8. Terma Revelations and Miraculous Events

Through the union of bliss, clarity, and nonconceptuality
you will achieve clairvoyance, extraordinary powers of perception,
and boundless qualities,
and ultimately you will achieve the wish-fulfilling three kayas
and all the qualities of the victorious ones,
spontaneously bringing about your own and others' welfare.
—Longchenpa*

On the eleventh day of the waxing moon Longchenpa sent the yogi Özer Gocha to fetch the texts of the Khandro Nyingthig. On Özer Gocha's return journey an aura of rainbow light permeated and surrounded them. And, during the night of his arrival at Chukpo Drak, near the stone stupas of Zurkardo, all the yogis and yoginis saw auras of five-colored rainbow light extending all the way from Chukpo Drak to Rimochen.

After first performing a ganachakra feast offering to restore and fulfill his samaya commitments, Longchenpa opened the door to the secret teachings of the Khandro Nyingthig. The highest forms of the gurus, yidams, and dakinis blessed him in order to fully reveal to him the great way in which the ultimate essence abides.

One can scarcely even hint at his experience with words that are normally used to point out the inner radiance. That night he knew the meditative clarity of resting in the state of the expanse of primordial purity, the dharmakaya; the sambhogakaya arose as its manifest expression of power; and the nirmanakaya and the six realms of samsaric existence arose separately as its

---

*Translated by Adam Pearcey in *Mind in Comfort and Ease*, p. 250.

outer radiance. In this way the dakinis blessed Longchenpa to nakedly see what was introduced.

It was then that he discovered the innermost esoteric Khandro Yangthig[1] as a mind terma treasure.[2] At the time, while he was writing down and revising these instruction texts of the Khandro Yangthig, the great master Guru Rinpoché Padmasambhava himself arrived in the guise of Thukdrup. A yogini, who possessed all the marks and signs of a dakini, also saw Yeshé Tsogyal to his right and Dorjé Yudrönma to his left dictating the texts.

Yeshé Tsogyal stayed there for six days, giving introductions and mind mandate transmissions of the signs and symbols, meanings, and examples of the Khandro Nyingthig, and entrusting these to Longchenpa. Because of this, many of the objects of meditation, ways of introduction, and unique ways of instruction—all of which were previously unknown and had never before been explained in written texts— spontaneously poured forth from Longchenpa's mind.

In the Land of Snow all of the other writings on the Nyingthig, even those considered profound, contain not even a fraction of the profound points that were extensively brought to light in this ocean of vajra truth, this mind treasure of Longchenpa. Having realized that what is found in these other texts is like a picture of a butter lamp that emits neither light nor heat, one should cherish well even a single verse of Longchen Rabjam's writings. Most of the instructions, in their early development, originated there at this time in Rimochen, but were later systematically arranged at White Skull Snow Mountain.[3]

During all of this, the key points of these teachings arose in Longchenpa's awareness, and when Yeshé Tsogyal herself appeared in her timeless awareness embodiment, he offered her an explanation of his direct understanding of these points. It was during this vision that Guru Padmakara[4] conferred the name Drimé Özer (Stainless Ray of Light) on Longchenpa, while Yeshé Tsogyal named him Dorjé Ziji Tsal (Vajra of Dynamic Brilliance).

As Longchenpa was preparing to confer the elaborate empowerment and was laying out the mandala, a red woman appeared and held the measuring thread. When the lines were about to be rendered, another woman whose hair was braided with gold and turquoise appeared and helped him draw the mandala.

During this first empowerment seven disciples gathered to receive it. Suddenly Longchenpa's nose began to bleed. Noting the significance of this, he said, "No more than three can enter this empowerment mandala. This bleeding is because there are too many people." Indicating four of those gathered, he said, "You four, go outside."

After the four had left, the room in which the empowerment was being bestowed was suddenly permeated with a glowing aura of rainbow light.

One of the students was taken over by the guardian goddess Namdru Remati, who in a boastful manner said, "Will you not give me an offering? I am the guardian of many hidden termas and have long endured this hardship." She then gave clear instructions on the details of the rites of herself and her entourage. She also gave a prophecy about an earth terma treasure for him to find, and displayed a great miracle. But Longchenpa declined, saying to her:

> As I have opened the doorway to the inner terma of clear light,
> I have no need of termas hidden in holes in rock faces.
> If I have termas, it's all right; if not, it's all right.
> If I am one with such good fortune, it's all right; if not, it's all right.
> For a yogin such as I, phenomena and ordinary mind have fallen
> away,
> So you need not try to buy me off with your arrogant boasts
> of guarding termas.

While Longchenpa conferred the background teachings and the precious secret introduction, everyone saw Yeshé Tsogyal take up the vase and grant the empowerment. They all immediately stood up and paid homage.

When he conferred the introductions to the bardo state, and to the penetration of the enclosure of inner radiance,[5] the dakinis were all delighted. He said, "Nonhuman beings value this doctrine more highly than do men, and they have greater aspiration and willpower. You should keep that in mind!"

Longchenpa directly introduced his students to the path of tögal without having to use traditional metaphors—such as "the light of a great, dark-blue expanse" and the so-called "lamp of totally pure basic space" and "lamp of empty bindus"—to illustrate the process.

When Longchenpa gave the introduction to the pristine awareness that is the inner radiance, the entire sky was filled with dakinis, their palms pressed together in prayer and reverence. That evening mantra protectress Ekajati actually descended and began to dance. The guru said, "This evening I am teaching the Nyingthig. Aren't you protectors of the transmitted precepts and the dakinis rejoicing?"

Ekajati answered, "All the dakinis are rejoicing. Guru Padmasambhava and Yeshé Tsogyal say of you, 'Where is there another like Longchenpa? He is marvelous indeed!' Above all, in Orgyen Dzong there is one delighted devotee."

Then the oath-bound protector Kyebu Chenpo[6] appeared by possessing one of the disciples and urged the master to set out for Orgyen Dzong. He also prophesied, saying, "You will have thirty disciples capable of serving the world. Among them, eleven will be great benefactors of living beings, and nine will be exceptional." To the disciples themselves he said, "You disciples are fulfilled by having met this guru."

Afterwards, when Longchenpa bestowed upon them the seal of entrustment of the Khandro Nyingthig, Shenpa Sogdrubma appeared and said, "Please don't recite my means for attainment."

Similarly, on the evening when he completed all the empowerments and oral instructions of the Khandro Nyingthig, the omniscient Longchenpa said to his disciples, "Yesterday the dakinis granted siddhis. Let's see whether they come again tonight. Mix some water with the chang." The disciples strained out the chang and filled a small pot.

"Isn't that enough?" they asked.

"No, that isn't sufficient. Mix in even more water, and strain it again."

And so they did as they were told, and all that they strained still remained potent, and the whole company became intoxicated. The guru said, "This demonstrates the reduplication and transformation of a single substance!"[7]

After that Dorjé Yudrönma urged Longchenpa to set out for her sacred place once more. When he consented she was filled with joy and said, "I will go on ahead!"

But then the goddess Remati possessed yet another person and implored Longchenpa not to go. Longchenpa replied, "Though I have given such teachings to you spirits, you do not understand; joy and sorrow are simply the machinations of ordinary mind. You may come wherever I am."

He then gave her an empowerment of contemplation, after which she responded, "I am most grateful and beholden to you."

"Where did you go yesterday?" he asked.

Remati replied, "I went to visit a herd of cattle in their pasture."

It was well known that at the time the cattle were suffering from an epidemic disease.[8]

Then the yogis and yoginis offered a mandala of their own clothes and wealth to the guru. They vowed to practice the teachings they had received, after which Longchenpa replied, "In this doctrine of mine, many will undertake to keep their vows of generosity and of practice."

After then giving the instructions on entering the enclosure of inner radiance he said, "These hidden innermost secret instructions of mine are rare in all of Jambudvipa. The worthy recipient who masters them will quickly receive the body of light."

Guru Rinpoché also instructed him to restore such places as the cliff of Lharing Drak, Orgyen Dzong, and the temple of Zha Lhakhang, and gave him permission to write treatises.

In the past Guru Rinpoché and his consort Yeshé Tsogyal had made two terma caches from the cycle The Union of Samantabhadra's Intent. They had concealed these in a stupa and in the capital of a pillar in the Chimphu uplands. In keeping with a prophecy Longchenpa received from the goddess Sarasvati and her four sisters, he revealed the second of these two cycles during his stay at Chimphu.

9. White Skull Snow Mountain

High among the mountains the mind grows clear and expansive,
the perfect place to bring freshness when dull and to practice
the generation stage.
Snowclad regions help make samadhi clear and awareness bright and lucid,
ideal for cultivating insight and where obstacles are few.
—Longchenpa*

WHEN LONGCHENPA RETURNED from Samyé Chimphu he performed a ganachakra feast offering at Chukpo Drak. The protectress Dorjé Yudrönma arrived there to welcome him. After that, when he was invited to Shuksep, a dakini took over the body of a yogini and asked the guru to please set out for Orgyen Dzong. And so he left for Özer Trinki Kyemotsel (Pleasure Garden of Clouds of Light) at Orgyen Dzong by White Skull Snow Mountain.

On his journey down from the uplands he was escorted by Dorjé Yudrönma, the twelve Tenma goddesses, and the gods known as the "nine Lharap brothers." When he reached White Skull Snow Mountain, he established his hermitage there, naming it Orgyen Dzong, and turned the wheel of the Dharma on a vast scale, teaching, for example, the Khandro Nyingthig to twenty-one fortunate students.

For this teaching, which is like the heart blood of the dakinis, White Skull Snow Mountain was most blessed. The hosts of the three roots and dakinis who gathered there were immeasurable.

At night the dakinis introduced him to the direct face of his true nature—of how the visions of clear light are embraced within the basic space of primordial purity, the enlightened intent of dharmakaya and how these visions

---

* Translated by Adam Pearcey in *Mind in Comfort and Ease*, p. 228.

manifest as the dynamic expression of being, and the arising of the sambho-gakaya appearances.[1]

Once there, in response to the prayers of the yogi Özer Gocha, he composed the supplementary texts to the Khandro Nyingthig[2] and revised and adapted his own mind terma treasure, the fifty-five treatises of the Khandro Yangthig. While he was composing the texts, the sky became filled with rainbows and marvelous events occurred. Everyone present saw the array of dakinis and countless magical events; rainbow light appeared and endless hosts of the three roots and dakinis gathered. They encircled Guru Long-chenpa, holding a parasol made of peacock feathers and adorned with a peak of precious jewels above his head.

Longchenpa wrote many of his major works, most notably the Seven Treasuries, at Orgyen Dzong at White Skull Snow Mountain. At dawn on several mornings he dreamed that Rigdzin Kumaradza pointed directly at him without saying a word; he interpreted this as a sign that he had received an empowerment.

Although there were indications that Longchenpa's death was imminent, he averted it during a single session of meditative absorption.

During this period, time and time again Longchenpa went and asked his guru, Kumaradza, to clarify his uncertainties about the instructions. Wherever he stayed he raised the banner of practice, to the delight of the guru.

Five times he offered all of what little he possessed to Kumaradza so that he could purify any clinging to material objects. In this way he honored his guru five times with offerings that were utterly pure with regard to the three spheres,[3] and also with two great offerings and seven utterly pure acts of devotion. He held ceremonies on the eighth, tenth, and twenty-fifth days of each month,[4] at which he pleased the pawos and dakinis with bountiful feast offerings and tormas.

Although the fame of his profound and vast scholarship and realization spread widely, he was neither attached to nor spellbound by appearances, and was free from both hope and fear of samsara and nirvana. And so he did not involve himself in the affairs of either monastery or household.

He had visions of countless yidams. Once, just as the first rays of the sun had broken over the horizon, Longchenpa heard a sound coming from the east. He looked up to see a mass of light, in the center of which was Saman-tabhadra surrounded by many mandalas of peaceful and wrathful deities filling the sky in all directions, above and below.

He also saw Vimalamitra, whose form was yellow-green, four gurus who had ascended to the pure dakini realm of Khechara, Kumaradza in sambho-gakaya garb, and Orgyen Pema Gyalpo.[5] As he gazed at these figures, the deities and gurus graced him with visions and uttered prophecies.

For example, in his vision Vimalamitra declared to him, "Simplify and summarize the meaning of my own Nyingthig teaching, the Vima Nying-thig, and teach it to your disciple Zhönnu Sangyé, who is the emanation of Kumaradza. He will have seven disciples bearing the name Zhönnu, all of whom will have the mantric syllable AH marked on the tips of their noses. They will preserve and spread the doctrine."

Through the blessings of the lineage gurus, coupled with his pure and diligent practice, he reached the citadel of the fully realized potential of awareness by the gateway of the all-surpassing inner radiance.[6] Henceforth, the experience of "awareness reaching full measure,"[7] a vision of the sponta-neous presence of clear light, arose continuously for him.

The true measure of this experience soon became obvious. His body could pass unimpeded through solid rock as though it were space; the slightest sound of his speech captivated the minds of discriminating individuals; and as repeatedly demonstrated by his vajra speech, his mind was imbued with the deep, indwelling confidence of realization.[8]

While Longchenpa was performing a fulfillment ritual of the peaceful and wrathful deities at Lharing Drak, he saw the mandala of these deities in the sky, complete with secondary circles within the main mandala con-figuration. When this had faded away, again Vimalamitra appeared in the southwest sky, pointed his finger southeast toward Zha Lhakhang in Uru, and declared that Longchenpa should restore the temple there.

At that same time, Longchenpa dreamed that Vimalamitra came to him, saying:

I am Kumaradza.
I have gone to the pure realm of Padmakuta.
Spread the seeds of the Buddha's teachings!

From this he knew that his guru, Kumaradza, had finally passed away. In an effort to finish carrying out the enlightened intent of his guru, Long-chenpa performed the dedication of total threefold purity[9] three times.

In addition, in order to guarantee that the teachings of the clear-light vajra essence would not wane, he completed the treatise entitled *The Precious Treasury of the Supreme Vehicle* in a very short time, using his miraculous powers to emanate numerous bodies and to bind the planetary mara Rahula to his service.

At Gyamane he gave the Nyingthig teachings to a gathering of many scholars, including Sönam Sengé and the master Lopön Palchok. When the time for questions came, he was asked if it was appropriate to engage in debate. He replied, "I will remain here for a month, debating with you over any sutras and tantras that you present to me." And so Longchenpa took on the academics and, with the lightning bolts of scriptural authority and logical reasoning flashing, he crumbled the towers of their arrogant pedantry.

Longchenpa lived his life as a hermit. He declined having any bureaucratic organization. Yet because of his impeccable scholarship and saintly nature, thousands of followers, including scholars, yogis and yoginis, as well as countless laypeople, flocked to him like moths to a flame. The greatest of scholars, as well as the highest politicians of the time, were deeply devoted to him. Because of their pure motivation they respected him for who he was spiritually, and never for power or influence, nor for any political or social gain.

The places where Longchenpa practiced, dwelling in total solitude with the sole purpose of attaining the heart essence of the teaching, included Samyé Chimphu, Orgyen Dzong, Lharing Drak, Trapu, Shuksep, White Skull Snow Mountain, Zhotö Tidro, Yerpa, Yarlha Shampo, Bumthang, Kyambu Pelgi Geding, Kongpori Lawalung, and Kongpo Tsagongphu. Most of all, he stayed at White Skull Snow Mountain. In Lhodrak, the Yoru region of Central Tibet, and in all the southern regions of Bhutan and its neighboring districts, his disciples would often gather by the thousands, and Longchenpa showed unbounded compassion to each and every one of them. He would accept no teaching fees, nor did he squander the offerings made by the faithful. He took part only in activities to benefit his disciples, and he patiently tolerated their faults and petty squabbles. Because of his respectful performance of many bountiful feast offerings and his intuitive sense of the minds of others, he would teach by using skillful means suited to his disciples' dispositions and capacities, and his enlightened activity was vast beyond description.

Now at this time[10] there was one called Gompa Künrin[11] of Drikung,[12] who was obsessed with pride in his own power and was preparing to wage war against Tai Situ[13] Changchub Gyaltsen of Phagmodru. Tai Situ Changchub Gyaltsen, a former Tripön of Nedrung in the ruling Sakya administration, was himself leading a revolt for independence against the Sakyapas' corrupt vassal government under the Yuan Dynasty Mongol "priest-patron" system. The Sakya lineage had been ruling Tibet since 1261, following Sakya Pandita's successful mission to the Mongol Khan.

The precious guru Padmasambhava had prophesied in his terma treasures:

> In the place known as Dri
> There will be a son of Mara named Kunga
> Whose body will bear a weaponlike mark.
> When he dies, he will go to hell;
> Yet if an emanation of Manjushri, coming from the south [of Tibet],
> Can subdue and convert him,
> He may be freed from taking rebirth in the hell realms.

When Gompa Künrin saw this prediction, he thought he recognized himself in these words. He examined his own body, and found that he had indeed a swordlike mark on his back. He knew then with certainty that he was the prophesied one. Though he was planning to wage war in Central Tibet (Ü) and the province of Tsang, he paused to reconsider, reasoning that little good would be achieved by his going to hell. So he made it known to everyone he trusted that he was seeking an emanation of Manjushri.

He appointed a special emissary on his behalf, a lama named Palchogpa, to search for Manjushri's prophesied emanation. At the time all the knowledgeable ones agreed: "In the four regions of Tibet there is at this time no one more brilliant than Longchenpa, the man from Samyé." So, after an extensive search, Palchogpa had no doubt that Longchen Rabjam was truly the emanation of Manjushri mentioned in Guru Padmasambhava's terma.

Gompa Künrin then invited Longchenpa to Drikung, where he served the Omniscient One with devotion and showed him every honor, offering him both the funds necessary to restore Zha Lhakhang and bestowing upon him the actual monastery of Drok Orgyen Gön. The master Longchenpa took Künrin under his care, giving him profound spiritual instructions, leading him on the path to liberation. At the time Gompa Künrin was the most powerful rival of Tai Situ of Phagmodru, so Longchenpa actually averted a serious war in Tibet through his wisdom and compassion.[14]

When Longchenpa journeyed through Tidro an escort of dakinis greeted him along the way and offered him that holy place. Shortly after that he arrived at Zha Lhakhang, where a white man wearing a white hat prostrated to him and pointed emphatically toward the temple.

DORJÉ LEGPA

From this, Longchenpa knew that Dorjé Legpa was encouraging him and that the time was ripe to begin the restoration. And so he did.

From among the numerous termas concealed within the cupola of the Zha Lhakhang temple, he extracted a full chest of gold from the back of the upper shrine, and many sadhanas of the twelve Tenma goddesses, Dorjé Legpa, and other deities.

When the earth was cleared away from the foundations, many evil skulls of different kinds were discovered; skulls had previously been placed there during a suppression ritual. Longchenpa reburied these, but as he began the suppression ritual demonic manifestations arose.

Earth and stones hailed down violently, a fierce wind blew, and a gloomy darkness fell like nightfall. His retinue was upset and dumbfounded; the experience was so frightening that some of his students just fainted on the spot, but Longchenpa himself chanted mantras wrathfully and assumed a menacing posture. Some of those present were able to have faith and perceive Longchenpa as the actual Guru Drakpo, the extremely wrathful form of Guru Rinpoché.

The skulls, which had been leaping about and clattering together, he crushed underfoot and immediately the manifestations disappeared.

Many such marvels occurred during the restoration of the temple. But there was one particularly remarkable phenomenon: every day a youth with a turquoise earring helped the artisans working on the reconstruction, though no one could tell where he went at night.

Curious about his unusual behavior, all of the artisans surrounded the youth. When cornered, he suddenly dissolved into a crack in the wall, disappeared, and was never seen again. They determined that this youth had been none other than the Dharma protector Dorjé Legpa. The oath-bound guardian deities plainly discussed the entire project—its successes and problems—with Longchenpa, just like people conversing aloud to one another.

Two pillars had previously toppled and there was no obvious way to raise them. Longchenpa recited a liturgy invoking the power of truth, and with his robe fanned the pillars, after which the artisans, to their amazement, were then able to easily set them aright to their original positions.

During the consecration ceremony numerous fortunate students saw Longchenpa manifest in the form of Samantabhadra, from whose heart rays of light shone; on the tip of each ray were buddhas surrounded by innumerable bodhisattvas, all casting down flowers.

To Longchenpa himself, the Lord of Sages, Shakyamuni, and the future buddha Maitreya appeared, surrounded by the sixteen elders of early Buddhism. Maitreya pointed at him and encouraged him, prophesying, "Two lifetimes from now, in the pure realm of Padmakuta, you will become the victorious one Sumerudipadhvaja."

10. Self-Exile in Bhutan

Whoever towards me generates anger or faith
or whoever hurts, praises, or follows me,
may I lead them all swiftly to enlightenment.
—Longchenpa*

Although Longchenpa's connection with Gompa Künrin had actually diverted Künrin from his plans to wage war against the Phagmodru faction of Tai Situ Changchub Gyaltsen, Tai Situ misperceived Longchenpa as his enemy because of his spiritual connection with Künrin, calling Longchenpa "the guru of the Drikungpas." As Tai Situ gained victory after victory in his battles against the Sakya government, and drew closer to becoming the new king of unified Tibet, his suspicions of Longchenpa increased, and he eventually sent forces to kill Longchenpa.

On the tenth day of the Monkey Month, Longchenpa beheld Orgyen Rinpoché amid a mass of light in the sky, surrounded by the luminous forms of dakinis of the five classes. When he had called together an assembly of some four thousand people, the dakinis of Tidro converged and took possession of many people. Through them they foretold many events, both positive and negative—for example, that at some point soon Longchenpa would have to go into exile in the Bumthang region of Bhutan.

He journeyed on in the area of Tidro and restored another holy site, which had recently fallen into disrepair, practicing a fulfillment ritual of the peaceful and wrathful deities for three weeks. Using his miraculous powers he went to places inaccessible to ordinary beings, where he planted victory banners and flags.

Later, when Longchenpa was staying at Shuksep, he had a significant

---

* Translated by Tulku Thondup in *The Practice of Dzogchen*, p. 176.

meditative experience. From behind the mountain, Jomo Karak, appeared the enormous head of a wrathful deity without a body, its eyes rolling and lightning shooting from its mouth.

Then another deity, Zadong Gongpo Rani, appeared, even more enormous than the first, with a black head, rolling eyes, and light shining from its mouth. These figures reached the summit of Jomo Karak and then vanished into an ascending stream of light. Longchenpa saw all of central and eastern Tibet covered by hail and a rain of rocks, with fork and sheet lightning flashing everywhere.

He understood that these visions were omens signifying the problems in Central and South Tibet, problems caused by political infighting between the Sakya and Phagmodru factions. He saw that a time of widespread social unrest was imminent, and despite his plans to restore a site at Yerpa and to build a mani[1] temple in Lhasa, he told his followers, "For the time being these projects cannot be completed. All of us, teacher and students, are going to Bumthang."[2]

On their way Longchenpa and his students passed through Lhasa, where the armies of Yarlung, the forces of Tai Situ Changchub Gyaltsen, surrounded and attempted to kill him. Longchenpa used his miraculous power to become invisible, thwarting his aggressors' attempt to harm him. They exclaimed, "Now where is he who was just here? Has he fled? He isn't here!"

That night while he was staying in an inner room and praying and making offerings to the Jowo image, he saw a light emerge from the forehead of the statue and dissolve into his forehead. As this happened he instantly and clearly recalled his former lives as a scholar at Vulture Peak in India and also in the country of Khotan,[3] and his knowledge of the vast range of scriptures of the Dharma that he had mastered at those times was awakened. Powerful experiences of bliss and clarity arose in his mind.

Within a mass of radiant light above the statue's head he saw the seven generations of buddhas, Bhaishajyaguru, the white and blue forms of Tara, Chakrasamvara, Hevajra, Avalokiteshvara (the form promulgated by King Songtsen Gampo), the thousand-armed, thousand-eyed form of Avalokiteshvara, and the deity Jinasagara.[4] In their midst stood the glorious protective deity Bernakchen,[5] the great guardian kings of the four directions, the Lion-Headed Dakini who protects against maras, and the glorious protector goddess Shri Devi. He beheld all of these in the space before him.

On the day he went to the Naga Cave in Drakra Longchenpa had a vivid vision of a huge mountain of crystal. That night he dreamed that he traveled to Mount Kailash, Tsaritra, and other holy mountains and saw for himself what they were like.

Next, when he arrived at the plain known as Poma Jangtang, he was met by an escort of the local spirits called the "twenty-one protectors" and the god Muri, who kept him constantly supplied with provisions. On the plain of Layak Mentang many fortunate students, headed by Khenchen Chabdal Lhündrup,[6] invited Longchenpa to stay for awhile and teach them.

Eventually, Longchenpa reached the Bumthang region of Bhutan in the south around 1350. There his karma continued to unfold, and he ended up staying there for ten years. He took up a residence at present day Samling Village below Tharpa Ling Monastery. Many disciples accompanied him, including his stable manager, who looked after his horses.

He soon discovered that there was no water around Samling and he thought of moving to another place. But one night five lovely dakini girls appeared in his dream and said:

> You aspire to live in this place;
> the lack of water should not deter you from staying.
> At dawn walk out of the house
> and we will show you the way to the water.

Longchenpa remembered the dream in the morning and followed the dakinis' instruction. To his surprise he saw a yellow flower in front of the door, though it was not in season. He walked towards the flower, only to find another flower, and then another.

Following the series of flowers led him along the ridge above Samling. When the flowers suddenly disappeared he looked around and found cattle footprints beneath a tree. As he removed the leaves around the footprints, water oozed out of the ground and soon filled the site like a lake. Longchenpa named the lake Nyenlam Zangmoi Tso (Auspicious Dream Lake). Auspicious Dream Lake is as large as the size of an average Bhutanese house. About three hundred feet from Auspicious Dream Lake in the direction of Urok Longchenpa found a waterfall cascading from a small cliff. The waterfall was very frightening and forbidding, and even today only a few people dare to approach it alone. It became a water source for the nearby villages of Urok, Rangbi, and Thrungbang, whereas Auspicious Dream Lake still serves as the water source for Samling Village.

Longchenpa brought the water from Auspicious Dream Lake to Samling through a small canal that he dug. Along ridges where canals could not be dug logs were carved with a "V"[7] to channel the water. The remains of old rotten or decayed log channels can be seen even now. Today at least thirteen water bubbles can be seen in the lake, signifying thirteen water spring sources. The nearby areas sometimes shake with the force of the water bubbling from beneath the lake. Due to his spiritual attainment Longchenpa thus brought forth springs of water and left many handprints and footprints in the rock near these sites.

During his long stay in Bhutan he founded a number of hermitages and monasteries, which became known as his "Eight Ling Temples": Tharpa Ling in Babron, Dechen Ling in Shingkhar, Tang Orgyen Chöling in Bumthang, Künzang Ling in Lhüntsé, Pema Ling (or Rinchenling) in Kothang, Menlok Künzang Ling in Wangdue, Drechag Ling in Nyenlong Valley, and Samtenling in Paro.

The first and most famous of his Eight Ling Temples was Tharpa Ling, above Samling Village, which he built in 1352.[8] There Longchenpa hid numerous pith instructions as termas in his bedroom, among these the cycle *The Union of Samantabhadra's Intent*, which he had previously discovered.

On one occasion over one hundred thousand devotees who had a wish for liberation gathered there to receive teachings from him. Later the eyes of a statue of Longchenpa in Tharpa Ling were deliberately made to look up to the sky. This was in accord with a popular legend that more than one hundred monks attained enlightenment in one day! Longchenpa, who was meditating in the lhakhang, looked up in the sky from the window and saw a hundred of his monks soaring in the sky.

The name and fame of Tharpa Ling spread throughout Tibet and many Tibetan devotees joined him at Tharpa Ling. The Tibetan border guards would not allow Longchenpa's devotees to pass if they simply said that they were going to Bhutan; but the moment they heard the name "Tharpa Ling," the border guards would stick out their tongues in respect and allow the students to proceed. In Tibet even the humblest monk coming from Tharpa Ling was entitled to a seat of honor since he was considered to be a geshé after having studied with Longchenpa. Such was the extent to which the fame of Tharpa Ling resounded even after Longchenpa later returned to Tibet.

Longchenpa's years in Bhutan were peaceful in contrast to Tibet, which was then rife with political conflict and strife. He wrote many of his major works while there in exile. On the summit of a mountain overlooking Tharpa

Ling and Samling there is a rock now known as "Longchen Zhugthri" where Longchenpa is said to have composed and written almost half of his epic work, the Seven Treasuries. While Longchenpa composed and dictated the texts from that rock, the planetary divinity Rahula, the mantra protectress Ekajati, and oath-bound Vajra Sadhu wrote the text and prepared his ink and paper!

While Longchenpa was staying mainly at Tharpa Ling, he often spent the summers in Tharpa Ling and the winters in West Bhutan at Künzang Ling.

One spring while Longchenpa was staying at Künzang Ling, and was preparing to return to Tharpa Ling in Bumthang, there were two lamas at Künzang Ling who were especially close to him. One of the lamas had a young daughter named Kyipala.[9] Kyipala wanted to devote herself completely to the Dharma, and she was particularly devoted to Longchenpa. At the time of Longchenpa's imminent departure she approached her father and said, "I really want to go with the master Longchenpa when he returns to Tharpa Ling this year. I really want to practice Dharma. I don't want to do anything else with my life." But her lama father objected, saying, "No. You are too young. You should stay here. Maybe next year, or some other time, you may go."

However, Kyipala replied that she did not want to wait; she really wanted to go; and she supplicated her father repeatedly with great insistence and determination. Finally her lama father went to Longchenpa and presented him with her request, asking the master if it would be all right for his daughter to accompany him on his return to Tharpa Ling. Longchenpa responded, "Yes, of course. Why not? If she is truly devoted and happy in the Dharma, if she really likes to practice, then she should come with me and deepen her learning, understanding, and realization." And so Kyipala bid her father and friends goodbye and went with Longchenpa to Tharpa Ling.

Kyipala truly applied herself to the Dharma, with the deepest respect and diligence, and became a very strong and faithful practitioner at Tharpa Ling. Recognizing her potential, Longchenpa took Kyipala as his secret consort. Kyipala, with the deepest devotion, love, and faith in Longchenpa, entered into this union with joy.

In 1351 Longchenpa had a daughter born to Kyipala and in 1356, a son named Gyalsé Tulku Drakpa Özer (or Dawa Drakpa), born in the Year of the Fire Monkey. Dawa Drakpa, also known as Thugsé[10] Dawa, as he is popularly referred to now, was a manifestation of the Dharma protector Hayagriva.[11] He later became a great scholar and practitioner and a holder of the Nyingthig lineage.

Longchenpa's son, Gyalsé Tulku Drakpa Özer, was born inside a cliff below the road between Tharpa Ling and Zanglai Pogto. His mother, Kyipala, used a large stone bowl to wash the baby with the water flowing from the cliff. This large stone bowl can still be seen today.

This water stream flows down between Samling and Zhitsar. There was a water mill on the stream near the river that flows through Chumé Valley. When all the other streams in the area freeze during the winter months and the water mills are idle, this particular stream, which has its source in the cliff, surprisingly never freezes and the water mill works all year round. The local people believe that the stream never froze again after it was blessed by the bathing of Gyalsé Tulku Drakpa Özer by the cliff upstream. The ruin of this mill is still visible today.

Longchenpa built a noble house (*nag tshang*) for his son Gyalsé Tulku Drakpa Özer in Samling, followed by a lhakhang.[12] Longchenpa's descendants can still be found in the Bumthang region of Bhutan.

Longchenpa entrusted the care of his horses at Tharpa Ling to his stable manager. Looking after the horses was a difficult job since Longchenpa did not have any pasture land of his own for grazing. The lands of Domkharpa, Urokpa, and Gyalsapa surrounded Samling from all directions. The stable manager would carry a packed lunch and go out to look after the horses every day while Longchenpa went about his own work.

Surprisingly, the people of Domkhar kept on complaining that Longchenpa's horses had been destroying their wheat crop in Pangri,[13] the land east of Samling. He found the complaints hard to believe since his stable manager was supposedly taking care of his horses.

However, Longchenpa wanted to get to the bottom of these allegations. So one morning when his stable manager was about to leave with the horses, Longchenpa stuck the end of a ball of thread on the back of his stable manager's coat using a needle, without his notice. As the stable manager travelled with Longchenpa's horses, unaware of the thread on his back, the thread ball began to unravel, leaving an easy trail for Longchenpa to follow.

Surprisingly the thread did not lead to the east, where his horses were supposed to graze, but instead led along the ridge above Samling. The thread led Longchenpa to a small lake called Shawa Bumpai Tso above Urok. Arriving there, Longchenpa was astounded to see various ritual objects and instruments strewn around the lake shore, and his stable manager, who was in the water swimming.

The stable manager's lower body had transformed into a snake. Longchenpa immediately recognized that his stable manager was not a man at all, but the Dharma protector Drasung Za Rahula.

Longchenpa made a sound when he accidentally stepped on some dry leaves. Rahula, on hearing the rustling sound and realizing that he had been secretly followed and discovered, quickly threw all the ritual objects into the lake. All Longchenpa could capture was a cymbal. Today this very same cymbal is kept in Samling as a revealed terma treasure.

Prostrating toward Rahula, Longchenpa explained that he had never known the true identity of his stable manager. The lake came to be known as Drasung Latso. Some time later Longchenpa built a zhakhang[14] for Rahula in Samling. There is a painting of Rahula done by Longchenpa, using his own blood, in the zhakhang.

So it turned out that the complaints made by the people of Domkhar were true after all. Following that event, the people of Domkhar developed a grudge against Longchenpa's neighborhood and started to revolt, much against the wishes and advice of the people of Urok, who revered him. The Domkhar king himself, Charalpa, led the revolt.

Longchenpa fled to the Dakpa region in eastern Bhutan. Before he left, Longchenpa made a prayer to protect himself against harm at the hands of the people of Domkhar. Following his departure it came to pass that for ten days and nights it was neither day nor night in Domkhar. In great consternation King Charalpa sought out astrologers and compelled them to divine the cause. Every divination pointed to Longchenpa.

At the time there were nine taxpaying households in Domkhar. King Charalpa summoned a man from each of these households and sent them to invite Longchenpa to return from Dakpa. The king threatened to throw them from Kayté Gangzam, a bridge across Chamkharchhu below Zhurkacé Village in Chumé, if they failed to bring Longchenpa back.

As commanded, nine men went to Dakpa and prostrated before Longchenpa. "Why did you come here?" Longchenpa asked.

"We come from Domkhar. Our king requests you to come back to Bumthang, and we came to receive you," they submitted. But Longchenpa refused, saying that the people had revolted against him once and that his life would be in danger if he should return.

"If you refuse, then we all are going to die before you; please make a prayer for us," they said, and explained their king's threat. They then threatened to commit suicide and asked Longchenpa to conduct an empowerment ritual for the deceased after they were dead.

"Well, it is surely better for me to return than for you all to die," Long-chenpa said, and out of compassion he acquiesced to their pleas. Long-chenpa then began his return to Tharpa Ling, following the traditional Dakpa-Bumthang route.

Before Longchenpa had escaped to Dakpa he had appointed a gomchen (a lay monk) as his regent in the small monastery he had built in Tharpa Ling. When his regent heard about Longchenpa's return, he became cov-etous and feared the loss of prestige and privileges he had enjoyed in his new position. So he requested a nun to kill Longchenpa by offering him poisoned tea and promised to give her a large piece of turquoise as a bribe. The nun agreed.

As Longchenpa was approaching Tharpa Ling, the nun crossed the gorge of Zanglaiteg and waited at Zanglaitegi Gor (Stone of Zanglaiteg), where the main road branches into two—the first one leading to Waters Hill and the second one to Tharpa Ling. There the nun met Longchenpa and offered him the poisoned tea on a huge flat rock.

"I will have to drink your tea. If I don't, you will not get the turquoise piece. But if I take it, I will suffer *this* pain," Longchenpa said, throwing the tea on the rock.

The rock instantly split into two. This huge rock, split from the middle, can still be seen in that spot today.

After Longchenpa's return, the people of Domkhar and their ruler, Charalpa, took an oath in a place called Portopong and swore that they would never again revolt, neither at that time nor in the future. The oath stone[15] testifying to their promise is still submerged beneath the earth in Portopong today. The king and the people then offered Longchenpa some meadowland in the place where his horses once grazed on their wheat. With this offering Longchenpa now was granted his own pastureland for his horses and his problems with the Domkhar people were ended.

The whole valley, the area that is now Urok Village, was by a big lake. The naga water goddess of the lake was afflicting the local villagers. There were a total of one hundred taxpaying households who had settled along ridges and slopes above the lake, and not one of the people dared to go near the water's edge. This made their life very difficult indeed, and finally the residents came to see Longchenpa at Tharpa Ling and beseeched him to subdue the naga.

Feeling compassion for their plight, Longchenpa went and meditated on a ridge above the lake called Portopong, located between Urok and

Samling. After nine days and nine nights of meditation on Tachung Nyenpa,[16] a horse's neigh was heard coming from Longchenpa's horse, which was standing beside him. The neigh reverberated across the valley and frightened the naga goddess, causing her to flee in the form of a snake. Longchenpa watched the snake escape towards Chumé. When it reached a place called Tonglakhag (below today's Sönam Künphen School), it turned and looked back at Longchenpa. The snake had a white face, and so the place was thereafter called *Dongkar*.[17] The grateful Urokpas became Longchenpa's patrons.

Longchenpa started an annual drubchen in Samling and the whole region came to join in the practice and ceremonies. The drubchen was held in the courtyard of Samling Noble Mansion (Samling Nagtshang) and it lasted for three days. On the second day the ter cymbal that Longchenpa had retrieved from Rahula was shown to the public. The cymbal was then struck to divine the luck of the people for the coming year. Good sound foretold an auspicious year for the people: cattle free from epidemics and diseases and a good harvest to come.

Lamas and monks who came from Samling Mansion were also the hosts; the people of Domkhar provided the dancers, the people of Gyalsa supplied firewood and water, while workers such as cooks came from Urok. The lead dancer (*champon*) had to be one of the nobles of Samling or a Samling lama, and the tail-end dancer (*chamjug*) had to be from the serfs. People who came for the drubchen had to be provided with free food. In later years Samling Mansion and Buli Lhakhang took turns in conducting the drubchen. It continued to be held alternately in Samling Mansion and Buli Lhakhang until Samling stopped the practice in the early 1960s. Today the drubchen is still held in Buli every two years.

Some time later Longchenpa offered to build a new zhakhang for his patron Dharma protector Rahula, and asked him to give any preferences he might have for the place. Rahula declared that his zhakhang should be built in a site where there was no dirty water from above, no smoke from below, and in a location where there is a stone structure in the shape of a swastika to the west.

After inspecting potential locations throughout the region, he finally selected Shingkhar Village as the site meeting all Rahula's stipulations perfectly. It was named Shingkhar Lhakhang. The first caretaker of Shingkhar Lhakhang was then sent from Samling, along with necessities and rations for his upkeep and needs. The present Shingkhar Dechenling Lhakhang[18] was built by Tsezang Thayé Drakpa, Longchenpa's great-grandson, who was the first Shingkhar Lama.

While Longchenpa was visiting the Mön region of Mangdé (Trongsa), he arrived at the present village of Shengleng in Baleng. There he gave teachings to the devotees, performed rites for the dead, for the sick, and other spiritual services. He built a lhakhang in Baleng as his winter residence and named it Shengleng Winter Lhakhang.

The local people, who were practicing Bön, were delighted to have such a great lama in their area. They became his patrons, and offered him about twenty *langdo*[19] of wetland[20] for growing rice; Longchenpa was to reciprocate the offer by visiting and staying at Shengleng Winter Lhakhang during the winter months. Moreover, Longchenpa had to sponsor the annual Samling drubchen with the rice harvested from the land offered to him. As agreed, Longchenpa visited the village each year during the winter, and also sponsored the Samling drupchen with the rice harvested from the land. The lhakhang can still be seen today.

From there Longchenpa went across a river to the next Mön village, called Wangleng. His visit coincided with the death of a local man, and the people requested him to conduct the empowerment ritual for the deceased. The people did not have anything of worth to present as an offering for the ritual, so they offered some of their farmland and pastureland.[21]

Once when he was to be received with honors in Menlok by Sönam Rinchen, a descendant of Drukgom Zhikpo,[22] Longchenpa flew from one mountainside to another to get there and back.

In these and other ways, displaying numerous unhindered miraculous powers, he tamed border regions where even the whisper of rumor about the Dharma had never been heard before. He introduced the practice of observing the ten virtuous actions and brought people to spiritual maturity and liberation through the Dharma according to each person's character. He subjugated malevolent nonhuman spirits—Chungdu, Dongzur Menmo, and others—and bound them to his service. Even today, the amazing deeds of the one remembered as Lama-la Ngawang Drimé Özer are recounted and held in the highest regard.

11. Return to Tibet

The main practice is the recognition of the natural state.
Through meditation involving bliss, clarity, and nonconceptuality,
the clear light primordial wisdom free from conceptual elaboration
arises as the fundamental innate mind.
—Longchenpa*

DUE TO THE power and influence wielded by the Drikung faction's resistance, Tai Situ Changchub Gyaltsen, who now, as Tibet's king, ruled the Phagmodrupa government, had earlier had little respect for Longchenpa, who he mistakenly assumed was Drikung Künrin's political ally.

Nevertheless, over time Tai Situ came to admire and revere Longchenpa's wisdom, realization, and activities. This change of heart was due in large part to the great and renowned master Sangyé Pelrin,[1] whose name was known to all ears, whose buddha activity flowed effortlessly from his great compassion, and whose life as a scholar and accomplished master was flawless and exemplary. Through this intercession Tai Situ finally realized that Longchenpa was impartial, had no interest in politics at all, and had actually averted further warfare by giving spiritual guidance to Tai Situ's foremost adversary, Drikung Künrin. Now even the great king Tai Situ became a disciple, and Longchenpa was able to return to Tibet after ten years in self-exile.

He was invited to Lhodrak[2] by its influential people, and in such places as Layak, Lhalung, and Dang-né he turned the wheel of the Dharma on a vast scale, transmitting the empowerments and teachings of the secret Nyingthig to gatherings of thousands, including such masters as Khenchen Chabdal

---

* Translated by Adam Pearcey in *Mind in Comfort and Ease*, p. 236.

Lhündrup, foremost among those requesting Longchenpa to return from Bhutan.

In Yardrok he taught the Dharma and was honored by the throne holder Tripön Dorjé Gyaltsen. On that occasion Gyalsé Zopa was explaining the Khandro Nyingthig to Tripön Dorjé Gyaltsen. Longchenpa told him, "It is excellent that you have received the Khandro Nyingthig from both Rinchen Lingpa in Kongpo and Lekdenpa in the region of Dakpo. But since I am the ultimate custodian of these teachings, if you have no pressing business elsewhere, stay a while and listen to my teachings. As the saying goes, 'If one sings the song one knows best on stage, it only becomes clearer.'" He then taught the Khandro Nyingthig to the throne holder and some fifteen students, and conferred teachings on a vast scale to many others gathered there.

At his seat in Yerpa the now reconciled Tai Situ hosted Longchenpa for a long time, showing him great honor. In turn, Longchenpa transmitted the Nyingthig empowerments and teachings to a gathering of about two thousand people. Tai Situ was awed by the superior wisdom of this Lord of the Dharma.

At Gongkar he cared for his students, Tai Situ foremost among them, by bestowing many empowerments and instructions. In the eastern part of Central Tibet he founded the monasteries of Kalden Jampa Ding, Yu Ding, and Pang Ding, staying at these places for as long as was appropriate; these became known as the "three Dings" of the Dra region.

In response to questions from the Sakya Lama Dampa concerning his methods of explaining the ground, path, and fruition, Longchenpa wrote a text entitled *A Petition: The Lamp of Gold*. In turn Lama Dampa offered the following verse to Longchenpa to please and honor him:

> This pleasant and totally illuminating speech
> is that of one who engages in explaining, debating, and composing
>   without confusion
> and who has the inner vision of scripture, reasoning, and numerous
>   pith instructions.
> To the yogin who has realized suchness, the essence of being,
> this verse is offered in this place of heaped jewels.

Furthermore, Longchenpa wrote many treatises on key points of the sutras and tantras in general, and on the Dzogchen approach in particular. For Drakpa Zangpo of Sangphu and other scholars he answered questions,

illuminating the subjects that their mundane minds could not easily comprehend, both directly, in the form of advice, and indirectly, in his emi-
nently well-reasoned essays and letters. He thereby inspired conviction in
others, who came to have faith in him and his teachings; thus he was given
the highly apt title "Künkhyen Chöjé (Omniscient Lord of the Dharma)."
Longchenpa was truly endowed with the qualities extolled by Dengom
Chödrak Zangpo in the following verses of praise offered to the master:

> When I beheld how Ngagi Wangpo explained the teachings,
> the methods of the "three brothers" seemed clumsy and halting.
> When I beheld the ordered reasoning of Longchen Rabjam,
> the teachings of Cha, Tsang, and Den seemed like nothing but
>   squabbling.
> When I beheld the works composed by the great Omniscient One,
> the works of Bu, Döl, and Shak seemed lackluster.
> When I beheld the view and enlightened intent of Natsok Rangdröl,
> the tenets of the "three great systems" seemed superficial.

Tai Situ sent him an invitation, but before Longchenpa could depart in
response to it, one of his students in retreat came to ask him a question. He
was so occupied throughout the day that he was unable to reply, but that
evening someone named Lama Zopa wrote a letter answering the question
and sent it off to Tai Situ.

During his journey Longchenpa was honored by Kyisho Sangdar, Yönten
Gyatso (the master of Sangphu), and others. While they offered him tea,
each of them asked a short question, to which Longchenpa gave a terse reply.
They were humbled by this and offered him presents, such as ten measures
of gold.

When he reached Lhasa, after his many years of self-exile in Bhutan,
Longchenpa was received by a procession of many monks. For a fortnight,
seated on a throne erected between the Jokhang and the temple of Ramo-
ché, he gave extensive teachings on the altruistic motivation and the bodhisattva vows, and conveyed transmissions on many other topics to a huge
gathering of people from all walks of life.

At Sangtsu Longchenpa used his peerless scholarship and realization to
humble many arrogant scholars learned in the Three Repositories.[3] Reduced
to confusion, they came to have faith in him. He made offerings in holy
places and gathered the accumulations on a great scale at many centers of

study and practice, dedicating all of these to the benefit of the teachings and the happiness of all beings. Journeying to Nyepu Shuksep, he brought more than a thousand fortunate people gathered there to spiritual maturity by teaching the profound approach of Dzogchen.

He predicted to a monk named Öndrakpa that the journey along the road to Upper Ur would take a long time, but that if the monk were to take a shortcut, his horse would throw him and he would be injured. It was with such unerring prescience that Longchenpa would speak of many things as obvious to him as they were hidden to others. Many of his students also received prophecies from dakinis.

At Khawari he was honored by Situ Shakya Zangpo, the myriarch of Upper Uru, whom he blessed with many empowerments and instructions. Situ offered enough provisions for him to stay through the summer, and then accompanied him on his travels, receiving teachings as they journeyed from the upland regions of Orgyen Dzong down to the lowlands.

Tripön Dorjé Gyaltsen, the myriarch of Yamdrok, and many other members of the nobility also showed their deepest respect and deference for the master.

Longchenpa conferred the empowerments, teachings, and background material of the vajra heart essence of clear light on more than three thousand people, including some forty masters who were teachers of the Dharma in their own right—including the scholars and students of Drikung—as well as many other important laypeople and monastics. He distributed many gifts and, on each tenth day of the lunar cycle, made offerings to all of the monastic communities from Penyül to Tsemogyal.

In his earlier years, whenever Longchenpa went into solitary retreat, before very long he would break his strict retreat and begin to teach, showing his clear understanding of all the source texts concerning Prajnaparamita, valid cognition, and so forth. Later, when his activities to benefit beings became more evident, he continued to teach in this vein.

For most of his life he tended not to stay in monasteries but in caves or under overhanging rocks or in huts made of grass and leaves, free of all the entanglements of retinue and personal wealth, spending his time entirely in practice. Of his love and appreciation for nature, he wrote:

> Far from the cities filled with entertainment,
> Being in the woods naturally increases the peaceful samadhis,

Harmonizes Dharma life, tames the mind,
And helps one attain the highest joy.

However, even when living in solitary hermitages, Longchenpa would still teach those fortunate people who were pursuing liberation. To groups ranging in size from a hundred to three thousand people he gave unflaggingly, and without sectarian bias, explanations of sutra and tantra texts, empowerments, and teachings commensurate with each individual's level of comprehension. He was unstinting in his efforts to serve the teachings, and particularly the teachings of Dzogpa Chenpo.

Thangka paintings and statues of Longchenpa usually show him dressed in fine brocade garments and wearing a pandita's hat, as if he were a wealthy lama. However, throughout his life Longchenpa lived very simply, gave away most of his possessions and offerings to support the Dharma, and was never one to spoil himself with ostentatious fine clothes and accoutrements.

On the tenth day of each month Longchenpa would offer two-thirds of whatever donations had come into his hands from the faithful, and use only the remaining portion for his immediate needs. When important or impressive people came, expecting to give him something, indifferent to their status he would refuse their offerings, saying, "I couldn't possibly accept this."

When passing out offerings, he would say, "Those of high status need never fear being overlooked," and would then proceed to distribute things, starting with those of lower status. He would say, "The Sangha—not wicked people—deserve honors," and he would never show any reverence, not even spreading out a sitting mat, to laypeople, no matter how high their social standing might be; again, his comment was, "Reverence should be offered to the Three Jewels, not to ordinary worldly beings. It is wrong to reverse the roles of lama and patron."

No matter how great the offerings his patrons made him, Longchenpa never thanked them; he would simply comment, "Let these patrons take this opportunity to accumulate merit rather than receive their repayment now in the form of gratitude." He would sometimes add, "This possession would only be wasted if they were to sell it," and he would never give his great patrons a gift in return. However, he was extraordinarily kind to poor, suffering, and humble people; he would show immense pleasure in the simple food and other gifts offered him by the poor, and would offer prayers of aspiration for them.

12. Final Days and Parinirvana

———

Life is impermanent like autumn clouds,
youth is impermanent like the flowers of spring,
the body is impermanent like borrowed property;
the lord of death, like the shadow of the western
mountain, will not delay.
—LONGCHENPA*

O N ONE OCCASION he conferred higher empowerments and special advice, as well as pith instructions and explanations of the tantras, on more than a hundred people who were capable of benefiting others with such teachings. Later he said to Gyalsé Zopa, "Close the door to the stairway and let no one enter while you take down this letter," and then dictated his last testament, *Stainless Light*, as follows:

Homage to all those exalted ones endowed with supreme compassion!
I pay homage to the one immersed in the experience of basic space, the
    primordial ground,
who cares for all beings through the proliferation and resolution of
    activities,
revealing a display in all its variety by the power of his innate
    compassion—a sublime sun, exceedingly and superbly radiant.

I pay homage to the one who, having completed his task in full,
went to a most superb and holy site, the town of Kushinagar,
to tame those fixated on the permanence of things.
I have come to understand the nature of samsara,

* Translated by Tulku Thondup in *The Practice of Dzogchen*, p. 177.

and because things of this world lack any true essence,
I now cast off this impermanent, illusory body,
so listen as I give this singularly beneficial advice.

We are, as it were, seduced by our belief that this life is real.
Things are by nature impermanent and without any real meaning,
so, having realized with certainty that nothing is reliable,
please practice the sacred Dharma from now on.

Friends and companions are like guests, in no way permanent.
Although they gather around you for a time,
all too soon you are parted from them,
so let go of emotional ties to your friends, who are like magical
    apparitions.
Please practice the sacred Dharma, a lasting source of benefit.

Wealth and possessions that you gather and hoard are like honey,
things that you amass but others enjoy,
so while you can, gain merit by increasing your generosity.
Please make preparations now for your future journey.

Your dwellings, well built yet subject to destruction, are like something on
    loan.
You have no power to stay when it is time to move on.
Give up completely your fascination with busy places,
and rely on a place of solitude from now on.

Liking or disliking is akin to a child's game.
Pointless attachments and aversions are a burning mass of flames.
Give up completely your quarrels and the malice you bear one another,
and tame your own minds from now on.

Actions, without true essence, are like magical illusions.
Although you strive at present, there is no final outcome.
Let go of the activities of this life and things of this world,
and seek the path to liberation from now on.

This body of freedom and opportunity that you have attained is like
    a precious ship,
granting you the power to free yourself from the ocean of suffering,
so give up laziness, lethargy, and procrastination
and arouse the strength of your diligence from now on.

The holy guru is like an escort accompanying you through a fearsome
    land.
To this guide who protects you from the enemy, samsara,
please show great honor, respect, and trust unflaggingly
with body, speech, and mind from now on.

Profound spiritual advice, like healing nectar,
is the most excellent cure for the disease of negative emotions,
so please rely on it in your life and cultivate it thoroughly,
gaining mastery from now on.

The three higher trainings, totally pure, are like a wish-fulfilling gem.
They are the path that brings happiness in this and future lives and leads
    to the most sublime goal.
Since they ensure enlightenment, the holy state of peace,
please apply them to your life from now on.

Teachings in all their variety are like a precious lamp,
banishing the darkness of ignorance and illuminating the path to
    liberation.
Since listening to them opens the eye of timeless awareness and sheds the
    light of benefit and happiness,
please be impartial and nonsectarian from now on.

Thorough contemplation is like the skill of a goldsmith,
cutting through all hesitation or speculation about what is or is
    not true,
so with the sublime knowing that comes from contemplating the
    nature of what you have heard,
please gain complete mastery from now on.

Meditation, by nature, is like tasting nectar.
To meditate on the meaning of what you have heard and contemplated
    pacifies all the illnesses of negative emotions.
You will cross the ocean of conditioned existence and arrive at the far
    shore—the heart essence.
Please meditate in the forest from now on.

View, by nature, is like clear open space,
free of all distinctions of high and low, all restrictions or extremes.
With no fixed dimension, it is beyond expression, imagination, or
    description.
Please use methods for realizing it from now on.

Meditation, by nature, is like a mountain or an ocean,
without transition or change, limpid and unsullied.
It pacifies all that characterizes distraction and conceptual elaboration.
Please meditate on reality just as it is from now on.

Conduct, by nature, is like a wise person,
aware of what is timely or beneficial in any situation.
Attachment and obsession, acceptance and rejection, repression and
    indulgence—these are of the realm of illusion,
so please be free of dualistic fixations from now on.

Fruition, by nature, is like the wealth a good leader takes possession of:
You, yourself, become wealthy and benefit for others is spontaneously
    ensured.
There is no hope or fear, only a mind that is automatically at ease.
Please endeavor to attain the fruition from now on.

Mind, by nature, is the basic space of phenomena, which is like the sky.
Space, by nature, is the ultimate meaning of the genuine nature of mind.
The supreme state is perfectly uniform, ultimately nondual,
so please realize it with certainty from now on.

Phenomena in all their variety are like reflections in a mirror.
They are apparent yet empty, with "emptiness" not to be found elsewhere.

In a cheerful frame of mind, without labeling phenomena as identical
    or separate,
please know this with certainty from now on.

Grasping at the objects you reify is like being in a dream.
Truth is nondual, for dualistic perceptions are caused by habit patterns
and are only labels applied by ordinary consciousness, empty by virtue
    of their very essence.
Please be aware of nonduality from now on.

Samsara and nirvana are, by nature, like the play of illusion.
Although things may appear to be good or bad, they are in essence
    equal.
Everything is unborn as the nature of space,
so please know this with certainty from now on.

Pleasant and painful perceptions based on confusion are, by nature,
    like phantoms.
Even as positive and negative causes and effects arise individually, by
    nature they are unborn, their essence without transition or change.
Please know this with certainty from now on.

Phenomena labeled by ordinary consciousness are like children's games.
In actuality they do not abide in a fixed way,
but through conceptual analysis people cling to particular philosophies
    about good and bad.
Please be aware of the equality of phenomena from now on.

Generosity, moreover, is like a treasure trove of jewels,
the cause of inexhaustible and ever-increasing wealth.
To all who provide an opportunity for you to gain merit—be they
    humble, great, or in between—please be generous, in whatever way
    is appropriate, from now on.

Discipline is like a noble, flawless vehicle,
transporting you to higher states of rebirth and the true excellence
    of enlightenment.

Whether avoiding what is negative, consolidating what is positive,
   or ensuring benefit for beings,
please apply discipline to your life from now on.

Patience is like a vast ocean, sublimely serene.
To remain undisturbed by challenges is the best of all spiritual qualities.
Accepting suffering, developing compassion, and so forth—
please become well acquainted with these virtues from now on.

Exertion is like a huge blazing bonfire,
incinerating what is unsuitable and feeding on what is positive.
Without succumbing to procrastination, apathy, or laziness,
please pursue the path to liberation from now on.

Unwavering meditative stability is like the most majestic mountain,
unruffled by any conceptual framework, undistracted by sense objects,
a state of equipoise, resting with whatever is the focus, not disturbed
   by anything.
Please cultivate meditative stability from now on.

Wisdom, vast in scope, is like the sun,
dispelling the darkness of ignorance, illuminating the sacred Dharma,
nurturing the garden of liberation, and drying up the reservoir of flaws.
Please see that it flourishes from now on.

Skillful means is like one who guides those seeking gems,
leading beings across the ocean of suffering to the Isle of Happiness.
All attain the three sublime kayas, and the two kinds of benefit are
   spontaneously ensured.
Please benefit others with skillful means from now on.

Fortitude is like a champion who defeats opponents,
vanquishing the hordes of negative emotions and bringing them to
   the path of enlightenment.
Since it perfects the accumulation of virtue and ensures freedom
   from obstacles,
please apply it to your life from now on.

Aspiration is like a great wish-fulfilling gem.
All wishes are spontaneously fulfilled, and supreme bliss flourishes
    as a matter of course.
To apply your mind to the state of peace is to have your hopes fulfilled.
Please develop aspiration to the highest degree from now on.

Timeless awareness is like the massing of clouds in the sky.
From the clouds of meditative absorption and complete recall fall
    the rains of benefit and happiness,
completely ripening the crops of amassed virtue for all beings.
Please endeavor to gain the experience of timeless awareness from now on.

Skillful means and wisdom are like a noble mount.
They prevent you from falling into conditioned existence or the peace
    of nirvana, and your own and others' benefit is certain.
You bring the five paths to consummation, and the three kayas are
    spontaneously present.
Please strive to accomplish skillful means and sublime knowing from
    now on.

Things that lead to enlightenment,
left in the wake of exalted ones throughout the three times, are like
    a great, fine road.
There are thirty-seven of these—the four bases of mindfulness and
    the rest.
Please endeavor to nurture them from now on.

Love, moreover, is like fine parents
who have unceasing sympathy for their children throughout the six
    classes of beings,
serving them with affection and always being of benefit.
Please cultivate love in your life from now on.

Compassion is like a bodhisattva, a child of victorious ones,
for whom the suffering of others is like his own
and who wears the armor of exertion in the quest to free them from
    this suffering.
Please apply compassion to your life from now on.

Joy is like the elder of a family,
who delights in the virtues of others
and rejoices in being able to provide for them.
Please become thoroughly familiar with joy from now on.

Impartiality, by nature like the level ground,
is free of affliction and of attachment or aversion to near or far,
supremely blissful, abiding invariably in the equalness of everything.
Please become naturally familiar with impartiality from now on.

The two aspects of bodhichitta are like a trusted guide,
leading all who are virtuous to the Isle of Liberation,
undaunted by conditioned existence and ensuring abundant benefit
    for others.
Please arouse them repeatedly from now on.

Devotion is like the huge reservoir of the ocean,
filled with what is virtuous yet of a single taste from beginning to end,
swelling with the waves of faith that never fails.
Please rely on devotion from now on.

Dedication is like the inexhaustible treasury of space.
By dedicating something within the basic space of phenomena
you guarantee that it will never wane but always increase.
Dharmakaya is the single taste within which the rupakayas are
    spontaneously present.
Please purify subject, object, and their interrelation from now on.

Rejoicing is like the realm of space,
embracing unlimited merit, without a fixed frame of reference, free
    of arrogance,
unwavering, and utterly limpid.
Please rejoice again and again from now on.

Mindfulness, moreover, is like an excellent hook,
holding the rampaging, untamed elephant of the mind,
drawing it completely away from what is flawed and bringing it naturally
    toward what is virtuous.
Please apply mindfulness to your life from now on.

Alertness is like a fine, undistracted watchman
who does not provide the thief, nonvirtue, any opportunity
but undertakes to guard the wealth of virtue.
Please rely on alertness with certainty from now on.

Heedfulness is like a surrounding wall and moat,
preventing the marauding hordes of negative emotions from invading
and marshaling the forces that emerge victorious over the enemy, karma.
Please strive to guard your mind from now on.

Faith, moreover, is like a fertile field
from which comes all that is wished for, where the harvest of
    enlightenment ripens,
and which ensures happiness in this and future lives, and benefit
    forever.
Please make certain that your faith flourishes from now on.

Benevolence is like a lovely pond of lotuses,
attracting what is sacred and delighting beings;
it is the very essence of the enjoyment of wealth and its rewards.
Please bring others happiness from now on.

Pleasant speech is like the sonorous drum of the gods,
never inappropriate, appealing to the minds of beings,
resonating for those to be guided, and arousing joy in them.
Please engender happiness by praising others from now on.

Calm deportment is like a holy sage,
inhibiting nonvirtue and arousing faith in others,
rejecting hypocrisy and ensuring a state of natural quietude.
Please adopt impeccable conduct from now on.

The sacred Dharma is like the powerful sugata,
appropriate for everyone yet far greater than anyone,
in harmony with everything, yet unlike anything else.
Please rely on the sacred Dharma from now on.

This body with its freedoms and opportunities is like an illusory mansion.
It is temporarily apparent, but will collapse with no warning.

There is no time to waste in this life, for phenomena are composite and
   will disappoint you.
Please bring this to mind again and again from now on.

Wealth is unreliable, like clouds in the autumn.
Good fortune will, by nature, decline;
there is no true essence at its very core.
Please realize this truth with certainty from now on.

All beings are impermanent, like guests who come and go.
The preceding generation has passed on, as will the younger in time.
Those alive today will be gone in a hundred years.
Please realize this with certainty from now on.

The experiences of this life are like those of a single day,
while the experiences of the bardo are like a nighttime dream.
The experiences of the next lifetime will come as soon as does the morrow.
Please practice the sacred Dharma from now on.

Having thus described all aspects of the Dharma metaphorically,
I have one more admonition for those with faith.
The end of all coming together is parting, so 'twill not remain, but will go
   to the Isle of Liberation. Since nothing in samsara is trustworthy,
please reach the continual state of authentic being, unborn dharmakaya.

The sensory appearances of this world are like cunning sorcerers,
by nature false, like a flirtatious coquette.
Since they rob the mind of its virtue and reinforce negative emotional
   patterns,
please cast them aside and practice the sacred Dharma.

If you have no contentment, you are poor though you may be wealthy,
for the mind of a miser is never satisfied.
Those who are content are truly the richest.
Even if they have little, their minds are filled with happiness.

Wine and women are sources of emotional affliction,
so cast off thoughts of desire, craving, and obsession.

Emulating the conduct of the sages,
cultivate the meaning of peace in solitary places.

It has been said, "Without tarrying day or night,
your mind focused on what is virtuous,
give up all that is injurious and bring about benefit."
So please practice the sacred Dharma without being distracted for a
    moment;
you will face death without regret and will benefit in the future.

One more thing, my students: we are connected through the Dharma
    and through samaya
thanks to our shared karma and pure aspirations over a very long time.
Although we have met, we must separate; master and disciples must part
    company.
Please understand that we are like travelers meeting in a marketplace.

I give this advice from my heart entirely to benefit you.
Homeland, wealth, dear friends, loving relations—
let go of all such distractions and complications of this life,
and please cultivate meditative stability in peaceful places.

When it is time for you to go, nothing will prevent it;
you need the sacred Dharma to meet death fearlessly.
From now on please exert yourselves in becoming familiar with the guru's
    pith instructions,
the teachings on what lies at the very heart of profound meaning.
Among all the teachings, those on the heart essence of clear light—
the secret meaning of the Nyingthig teachings—lie at the core of
    everything.
They are the most sublime of all, the path to buddhahood in a single
    lifetime.
Please endeavor to accomplish this wholly positive state of supreme bliss.

Furthermore, seek teachings from the holy ones of the lineages
who hold the quintessential nectar of profound meaning.
Use the strength of your diligence to practice these in solitude.
Then you will swiftly attain the state of a victorious one.

The sacred Dharma ensures complete, sublime bliss from now on
and benefit into the future.
Not all of its qualities may be immediately apparent,
so please exert yourselves from now on in order to realize the meaning
    of the heart essence.

The lord of the stars, the moon unobscured by clouds,
replete with all the qualities of fullness, is on the point of rising.
Canopies, parasols, victory banners, the sound of music, and the gathering
    of hosts of dakas and dakinis make everything so beautiful.
The lotus visage of the protector, the embodiment of compassion who
    takes me under his care, inspires me.

Now it is time to depart, like a traveler journeying on the open road.
The joy I feel at dying is my finest accomplishment,
greater by far than that of any merchant who has gained an entire ocean
    of wealth,
or that of Indra, lord of the gods, who has emerged victorious in battle,
or that of anyone who experiences bliss by achieving meditative stability.

Now I, Pema Ledrel Tsal, will not linger,
for I go to assume the stronghold of immortality and supreme bliss.
This life, my karma, the momentum of my aspiration, my worldly
    concerns,
the perceptions of this lifetime—all have come to an end.
When the panoramic visions of pure realms arise in the bardo,
I will be aware, instantly and spontaneously, that in essence these are
    awareness's own manifestations
and that I am therefore close to attaining the ongoing and authentic being
    of the primordial state.

Because I am truly blessed, you and others should be happy.
Use this illusory lifetime to attain the goal, the Isle of Liberation.
It is my aspiration that we will then meet again, my holy disciples,
and that we will be gladdened, rejoicing in the Dharma.

But for now, our connection in this life has ended.
Do not lament the passing of this wandering beggar who is happy
    with his lot.

Instead, pray to him constantly.
These are my words of advice, offered for your benefit,
like a multitude of lotus flowers delighting the bees—you, my faithful
    ones.

May the virtue of these well-chosen words ensure that those in the three
    realms
pass into nirvana on the level of primordial being!
This concludes my testament, *Stainless Light,*
advice from Drimé Özer.

Longchenpa thus composed both this testament, *Stainless Light,* and one entitled *The Mirror of Key Points* and included them in the collection of the Khandro Nyingthig.

When he had revealed this testament, Gyalsé Zopa cried out, weeping, "Please, don't talk like this!" At this point, the guru spoke at length and in depth on many topics, starting with the impermanence and decay of all transient things.

Soon after, while he was celebrating a ganachakra with his students, he encouraged them repeatedly, saying, "All of us, master and students alike, have only this evening to share teachings and celebrate this ganachakra. Those of you capable of benefiting others should care for fortunate students, bestowing empowerments, explaining the tantras, and transmitting pith instructions, without any thought of your own vested interests.

"Those of you who are pursuing personal practice, rest in equipoise according to the approaches of trekchö and tögal without becoming caught up in worldly activities. If at certain times there are things you do not understand, consult my work *The Innermost Heart Essence: The Wish-fulfilling Gem.*[1] It truly is like a gem that fulfills wishes and provides all that is desired. Examine it carefully and extract the very essence of lasting bliss in meditation."

Having given this advice, Longchenpa left for the temple of Zha Lhakhang, where he made offerings and prayed. As he was teaching to a crowd a marvelous rain of flowers fell. He continued in stages to the monastery of Orgyen Gön, where he remained for a brief time.

Upon departing, he said to those present, "I will not bother you any longer," and continued on to Chimphu. Along the way he was met by an escort of students and patrons from Gyama. He chided them, saying, "All of you, go back! Don't come to me out of worry. None of you will see me after this. You should instead exert yourselves in practicing the Dharma."

When he arrived at the forests of glorious Chimphu, he observed, "This holy place is just like the charnel ground of Sitavana in India. I would rather die here than to be born elsewhere. Here I will leave this worn-out illusory body of mine, right here at this charnel ground."

But as Longchenpa was preparing to pass into the rainbow body, Vimalamitra and Ekajati both appeared to him and requested that, for the sake of beings, he gather his disciples in a vast assembly and give them his final teachings and transmissions, that he once more display his miraculous concerned activity in a great gathering rather than transfer to the rainbow body in solitude.[2]

And so he went to Samyé upon the invitation of its six stewards and taught the unsurpassable secret doctrine to a large gathering. Because there were so many people, the unelaborate empowerment took a number of days, during which Longchenpa, who had fallen ill, grew progressively sicker.

Then, on the sixteenth day of the month, he said, "Set out offerings for a ganachakra. I shall perform an empowerment."

"But you are ill; that would be tiring," his attendants protested. "You should rest for a few days."

He replied, "It is not necessary for me to rest. I will finish these empowerments. I have decided to teach this doctrine completely."

Thus, on Saturday, December 23, 1363[3] (the sixteenth day of the twelfth month of the Water Hare Year), he delighted the dakas and dakinis with bountiful worship and offerings. He then spoke most sincerely to his close disciples, again saying, "Since all compounded things are insubstantial, you should devote yourself entirely to the Dharma. In particular, you should focus on achieving practical experience of the highest esoteric instructions of trekchö and tögal. If sometimes you find that you don't understand, then look minutely and meditate on *The Innermost Heart Essence: The Wish-fulfilling Gem*, which is truly like a jewel that grants all your desires. Then you will attain nirvana at the level where reality is exhausted."[4]

At the age of fifty-six, at midday on Wednesday, January 24, 1364 (the eighteenth day of the twelfth month of Gyal in the Female Water Hare Year[5]), Longchenpa instructed Ösel Rangdröl, Künpal, and the others who were attending him to set out offerings and leave him alone. They prepared and arranged the offerings but then asked permission to stay.

"All right. I am getting ready to cast off this broken-down, worn-out illusory body; stay if you will, but don't make a fuss. Be quiet, and rest in meditative equipoise."

He then adopted the dharmakaya posture, and he set his intention to rest in the primordial expanse of dharmata. In accordance with the request of Vimalamitra and Ekajati, he did not transfer into the rainbow body, although he certainly could have, and had been ready to do so. In his life, he had achieved complete realization by merging his awareness in the exhaustion of all phenomena as primordial purity. Thus, at this time of passing, he displayed the attainment of trekchö, which he manifested directly in the bardo of dharmata. At that time he achieved the state of fully manifest, perfect enlightenment as a buddha.[6]

Because of his accomplishment there were limitless miracles that occurred. Those present felt the whole earth tremble and shake, and heard roaring sounds. The gods who take joy in the teachings spread forth a canopy of shining rainbow light in the clear sky and made a rain of flowers fall. Some of the faithful people present for his passing experienced a stable realization of clear light.

These and other marvelous signs continued to manifest throughout the month of funeral ceremonies. While Longchenpa's remains were kept in state, undisturbed for twenty-five days and venerated, a marvelous and exquisite odor more fragrant than sandalwood or camphor was perceptible everywhere, and the tent of rainbows arched constantly across the sky.

When his intention finally dissolved into the dharmakaya, even the four elements bowed to him by departing from their usual sequence; the earth grew warm although it was in the time of the twelfth to first months; the ice melted unseasonably, and wild roses and other flowers bloomed.

As his remains were taken to the pyre, the earth shook three times and a mighty thunder resounded seven times. After the cremation his heart, tongue, and eyes—the signs of his having awakened to the three vajras of body, speech, and mind—were unscathed by the fire, and fell into the laps of his fortunate disciples. Because he had realized all that can be accomplished with respect to the five kaya bodies of buddhahood and the five pristine wisdoms, many ringsel,[7] and five kinds of dungchens[8] were found in his ashes. The larger relics multiplied by the hundreds and thousands, seemingly without limit. Up to the present day, those who possess even a tiny fragment of his undamaged relics cannot be afflicted by the "upper demons."[9]

In addition, his skull survived intact, yellowish white and as hard as stone, by nature a holy relic. Also, relics representing the five buddha families and countless smaller relics, along with many images of Amitayus and other deities, were discovered in the ashes.

A statue of Longchenpa as an inner support, a stupa of complete enlightenment as an outer support, and other structures were later erected on that very spot.

Thus did the incomparable Longchenpa live, and thus did he pass from this world. Thus did the Omniscient Dharma King Longchen Rabjam Drimé Özer guide others with the enormous merit of his physical embodiment. Thus have the merits of his teaching, vast writings, practice, and example continued to benefit countless beings to this very day, serving in the darkness of these degenerate times as a beacon of unfailing truth.

13. His Legacy

May my happiness be experienced by all beings,
May the sufferings of living beings be transferred to me.
Until samsara is emptied,
May I lead living beings.
—Longchenpa*

His Prophesied Rebirths

Gyalsé Tulku Drakpa Özer

LONGCHENPA'S FIRST REBIRTH appeared while he was still alive, manifesting as his own son, Gyalsé Tulku Drakpa Özer. His story unfolds later in this chapter.

Pema Lingpa (1450–1521)

Longchenpa's next rebirth was as Pema Lingpa, recognized as the fourth of the five "tertön kings," or treasure-finders.[1] He was the last of the five pure incarnations of King Trisong Detsen's daughter, the royal princess Pemasal.

Since, in his previous life, he had been the omniscient Longchen Rabjam, who had attained supreme realization, Pema Lingpa came into this world fully enlightened. Born amidst auspicious signs and omens in the year 1450 in Bhutan's Bumthang Valley, Pema Lingpa was a descendant of tantric practitioners of the Nyingma order. His father was Töndrup Zangpo of the Nyo clan; his mother was Trongma Peldzom of a nomadic clan.

From a young age he lived with his grandfather, the blacksmith Yönten

---

*Translated by Tulku Thondup in *The Practice of Dzogchen*, pp. 176–177.

PEMA LINGPA

Jangchub, and his grandmother, Ani Döndrup Zangmo, at Mani Gompa. The tertön Dorjé Lingpa once told his grandfather, "Blacksmith, this boy of yours will be of great benefit to the Dharma and to beings." As a child he had a commanding and confident presence, and chose his course in life early on. Even at play he would sit on a throne and act as if he were giving teachings and empowerments to his playmates; he would gather an entourage, chant mantras, perform sacred dances, and enter into meditative absorption.

By the age of nine all fields of learning became effortless for him, whether it was reading and writing or ironwork and carpentry. In this way he mastered various texts, crafts, and much else without needing instruction.

His formal religious training was not extensive, but from his young adult years on he received instructions through his dreams and visions that he was to extract 108 terma treasures from throughout Bhutan, as well as in Tibet and parts of India. It was not long before his foretold destiny as a tertön came to ripen and manifest.

In his twenty-sixth year, on the tenth day of the seventh month of the Fire Monkey Year, 1476, in the place called Mani Gompa, a mysterious monk appeared, handed him a paper scroll, and then disappeared without a trace. Looking at the scroll, it read, "On the night of the full moon this month go to the place called Long-Nosed Lion Cliff at the bottom of your valley. There lies your destined treasure. Take five friends with you and retrieve it!"

And so, when the full moon night arrived, Pema Lingpa convinced five friends to accompany him to Long-Nosed Lion Cliff, where the Tang River of Bumthang flows by the famous Burning Lake (Mebartso). As Pema Lingpa arrived at the edge he lost all bearings; he then took off all his clothes and leaped into the water.

Beneath the surface of the water he saw a life-sized statue of the historical Buddha Shakyamuni within an underwater cave called Glorious Long Cave. On the left side of the figure was a stack of many rhinoceros-skin chests. A one-eyed woman dressed in maroon clothes[2] handed him a chest that contained the text *The Quintessence of the Mysteries of the Luminous Space of Samantabhadri.* Then he was mysteriously propelled back onto the cliff, whereafter he returned home with his friends at midnight.

Once back at Mani Gompa, when it was time to transcribe the yellow treasure scrolls, his ink ran out. Instantly a dakini appeared and offered him a self-filling pot of ink, and then made prophecies about Pema Lingpa and other events as well. Later, when he first opened the door of the ripening empowerments and liberating instructions of this sacred teaching, many auspicious signs appeared, such as a canopy of rainbows and a rain of flowers. And each night he experienced Padmasambhava and Yeshé Tsogyal explaining to him the exact details of how to perform the empowerments and give the instructions, how to perform the dances, the musical notation for the ritual activities, and he would implement these instructions precisely on the following day.

That same year, on the fourteenth day of the eighth month, he brought forth from Burning Lake the second of the profound treasures of this inventory: the Cycles of the Luminous Expanse of the Great Perfection.[3] With a large crowd gathered at the edge of the water, Pema Lingpa held up a burning butter lamp in his hand, declaring, "If I am a demonic emanation, then may I die in these waters! If I am the son of Orgyen, then may I find the necessary treasures and may this butter lamp not go out!"

After saying this he jumped into the deep water without hesitation, holding the burning butter lamp in his hand. The crowd had various reactions and a clamor arose, but almost immediately after, Pema Lingpa shot glistening from the water, the lamp in his hand still burning! He carried under his other arm a buddha statue and a great skull chest that contained a terma treasure. Everyone in the crowd was astonished, and convinced of his extraordinary qualities they developed unshakeable faith; many actually experienced liberated awakening. After that, Pema Lingpa's reputation covered the Land of Snows like the sun and the moon.

In a similar miraculous way he discovered The Great Perfection: The Union of Samantabhadra's Intent at Samyé Chimphu, the holy area near Samyé Monastery. From these two treasure sites he subsequently brought forth many other treasures that are included in the essential practices of the Nyingma lineage to this day.

Throughout his life Pema Lingpa extracted a multitude of sacred objects, such as statues, texts, and stupas. He discovered the flesh of one born seven times as a Brahmin, which grants liberation upon taste.[4] He also discovered several terma images of Guru Padmasambhava. In addition, he uncovered the temple of Lho Kyerchu, which was similar to the temple of Peltsap Sumpa at Samyé, and which had not been visible previously; it can still be seen today.

Among the riches Pema Lingpa discovered were the life-supporting turquoise gems of the Dharma King Trisong Detsen, the seamless robes of the Princess Pemasal, a clairvoyant mirror, and many other sublime riches of the royal dynasty.

His vast enlightened activities attracted a following of ordinary folk as well as many significant political and spiritual figures of his time, including the Seventh Karmapa, Chödrak Gyatso. His qualities were extolled by all four of the main lineages of Vajrayana Buddhism. Pema Lingpa spent most of his life revealing the unexcelled treasures of Guru Rinpoché, meditating in isolated locations, granting empowerments and teachings, building and restoring monasteries, and generating a tradition that endures to the present day.

Although Guru Rinpoché had placed in his hands an inventory of 108 treasures, Pema Lingpa only revealed thirty-two of them due to the karmic disposition of beings at that time. And so, when the tertön was approaching death, his son asked his permission to find and reveal the others. The master replied, "It will be hard for you to find the treasures, but if you purely guard your samaya commitments and pray to me, you may perhaps find a few minor ones." Accordingly, his spiritual son, Dawa, brought forth some of the treasures.

The thirty-two treasures that Pema Lingpa was able to reveal contain the essence of all 108 treasures, summarized in the cycles of the three heart practices transmitted to Princess Pemasal by Guru Rinpoché: Lama Jewel

Ocean, The Union of Samantabhadra's Intent, and The Great Compassionate One: The Lamp That Dispels the Darkness.

The vast and wonderful deeds of Pema Lingpa, of liberating and benefiting immeasurable beings, were inconceivable. He prophesied that he would become a future buddha named Vajragarbha in the Buddhafield of the Lotus Array, and that all those currently associated with him would be reborn in that realm as well and become the disciples of that buddha.

There is also another prophecy among Pema Lingpa's revealed treasures concerning the host of disciples who became his spiritual sons:

> Ten thousand will be associated by past deeds.
> One thousand and two will be associated by aspiration.
> Those associated through the profound essential point will
>   be eleven.
> Seven will be mandala-holders.
> And three will be spiritual sons, dear to his heart.

In fulfillment of this prophecy a great number of disciples appeared. Among them, the foremost included six treasure-finders who were emanations, six greatly accomplished masters, and six great sons who manifested the signs of accomplishment. Tsultrim Paljor, Nangso Gyelwa Tondrup, and Tulku Chokden Gönpo were the three spiritual sons whose realization was the same as that of Pema Lingpa himself. Among his four sons, his spiritual son Dawa, who was an emanation of Avalokiteshvara, had profound powers of blessing and his enlightened activities were very extensive. He became one of Pema Lingpa's main lineage holders and was honored by numerous great masters throughout Tibet.

The transmission of Pema Lingpa's profound treasure teachings was gradually passed down and propagated by Tulku Natsok Rangdröl and Umdzé Töndrup Palbar, renowned as incomparable doctrine-masters, and by Sungtrul Tsultrim Dorjé (also known as the emanation of his spiritual son Dawa), who occupied a seat at the Lhalung Monastery in Lhodrak. Pema Lingpa's lineage has since spread throughout Bhutan and Tibet.

Today Pema Lingpa's lineage is especially carried on through three lines of body, speech, and mind emanations: the Gangteng, Sungtrul, and Tuksé Rinpochés, respectively, all of whom currently reside in Bhutan. Gangteng Tulku Rinpoché, the abbot of Gangté Gompa, is the ninth body incarnation of Pema Lingpa.

Thus, the entire lineage of Pema Lingpa's discovered treasure empowerments, transmissions, and instructions has continued, unbroken, through the guidance of a number of great masters up to the present day.

LONGCHENPA'S LINEAGE-UPHOLDING DISCIPLES

Longchenpa's foremost heart son disciples who tasted directly the nectar of his enlightened speech were: the "three learned and accomplished ones," who became famous: Khenchen Chabdal Lhündrup, Khedrup Delek Gyamtso of Zhoktarling, and Khedrup Chökyi Drakpa. Also, his successors included his "five heart sons," namely Dengom Chökyi Drakpa Zangpo of Dokam, Gyalsé Zangpo Drakpa Zopa, Lama Palchok, Guru Yeshé Rabjam, and Zhönnu Sangyé. There were also four disciples known as "the four spiritual benefactors who spread the teachings": Tulku Paljor Gyatso, Lopön Sangyé Kunga, Lopön Lodrö Zangpo, and Takgo Jadrel Chöjé Tashi Jungné.

Another four were called "the four accomplished yogins," namely Phago Tokden Gyalpo, Naljorpa Özer Gocha, Rigdzin Ösel Rangdröl, and Jatang Sönam Özer.

In addition, Longchenpa taught many masters such as Trulzhik Sangyé Önpo, Orgyen Chöjé of Drok, and Khenpo Sönam Sengé of Lu. Moreover, there were many spiritual benefactors who were holders of his teaching, such as Sangyé Pelrin, who had reconciled him with the lord of Neudong (Tai Situ), and Drakpa Pal, as well as thousands of others who received the complete transmissions of empowerments, commentaries, and the oral pith instructions.

Those who received some empowerments were countless, many of whom gained a true measure of meditative experience and accomplishment. Thus, through Longchenpa's generous and tireless sharing of his Dharma wisdom, the hills and valleys of Tibet became filled with practitioners meditating on the Great Perfection—Dzogpa Chenpo.

From his many excellent disciples there were, in turn, many lineage branches that sprang from the great river of Longchenpa's teachings. Following but one of these major branches, we begin with Khenchen Chabdal Lhündrup.

Khenchen Chabdal Lhündrup (fourteenth century)

As previously described, Khenchen Chabdal Lhündrup first met and received teachings from Longchenpa when the guru was on his way to self-exile in Bhutan. At that initial meeting Chabdal Lhündrup became certain that the great Omniscient One had been his guru in previous lives, and served Longchenpa with devotion, perfectly displaying the three kinds of faith.[5] Longchenpa brought him to spiritual maturity with the Nyingthig teachings and other instructions of the profound path of the unsurpassable secret.

After Longchenpa had departed to continue on his way to Bhutan, his new disciple Chabdal Lhündrup built himself a retreat hut at Zekhar, a hermitage in Lha Valley, and spent five years practicing the clear-light Dzogchen yoga without interruption or distraction. He eventually reached a definitive realization of the Great Perfection, seeing rigpa's natural appearances without accepting or rejecting.[6] He had visions of many yidams and numerous dharmapalas, such as Vaishravana, listened to their commands, and carried out their enlightened activities. He was able to see into the future and his predictions came true as foretold.

Khenchen Chabdal Lhündrup was also first among those to invite the Omniscient Longchenpa to return from Bhutan, receiving him in Lhodrak, where they requested that Longchenpa turn the Dharma wheel on a vast scale. There, among other teachings, Chabdal Lhündrup received further teachings on the Khandro Nyingthig, and later wrote commentaries based on his questions about the transmissions he had received previously from Longchenpa and the answers that he received from the Omniscient One. The guru was very pleased; he accepted Chabdal Lhündrup as his heart-son disciple and entrusted him as a lineage holder, saying, "Pass this on to my son, Drakpa Özer!"

He lived to the ripe old age of ninety-seven, when his emanated form resolved back into the dharmadhatu. After keeping his remains in state for a month, when they were cremated many relics were found in the ashes, and many other miracles took place that instilled great faith in everyone present.

Gyalsé Tulku Drakpa Özer (1356–1409)

Chabdal Lhündrup's main disciple was Gyalsé Tulku Drakpa Özer, Longchenpa's own son. As is said in *The Golden Garland of Questions and Answers* from the Khandro Nyingthig cycle:

> The next incarnation of Ledrel Tsal
> Will remain for a short time in a sambhogakaya pure realm
> And will then take birth at Tharpa Ling in Bhutan.

From the age of fifteen he will benefit beings.
Then the son, Dawa Drakpa, an emanation of Hayagriva, will appear;
He, too, will benefit beings.

In fulfillment of this prophecy, Longchenpa, the Omniscient Dharma King, attained a sambhogakaya pure realm, for he had experienced the third vision of tögal, the full expression of awareness as the spontaneous presence of clear light. From that state he manifested as his own tulku while he was still alive, in order to guide beings in the form of his own son, born from his consort Kyipala.[7]

At a later date Longchenpa appeared in a vision to the master of the doctrine Drikung Rinchen Phuntsok and declared that he, Longchenpa, had been reborn as his own son, Gyalsé Tulku Drakpa Özer. Longchenpa's hat was placed on Tulku Drakpa Özer's head and he became a direct disciple through that blessing.

When he was still very young Drakpa Özer felt the qualities of someone holy awaken within him. He sang songs of advice to his mother, and would explain the meaning of the Dharma to all who came near. At this time, many people saw the great mantra protectress Ekajati holding him in her lap and the seer Rahula guarding him.

Throughout his life Tulku Drakpa Özer was boundlessly dedicated to maintaining, preserving, and propagating the scriptures of his father, Longchenpa, in Tibet and Bhutan, where he illuminated the path to liberation with the torch of Dharma, including the teachings of the vajra heart essence of clear light. He became a great master who blessed all of the places where he stayed, pacifying illness, famine, warfare, and social unrest, as well as many other problems of the people.

He took the lady Machig Gyaltsen Bum as his consort and from their union two sons were born. The elder son, Nyima Özer, was asked to become the protector of his father's students in the northern parts of Uru within Central Tibet. There he created great benefit both by teaching the Dharma and continuing the family line. Their second son, Dawa Drakpa, was to become a great lineage holder himself, as will be described later in this chapter.

At the age of fifty-four Tulku Drakpa Özer passed away at Kalden Jampading. When his remains were cremated, all those present were moved to faith by amazing signs, such as many relics and images of deities found in the ashes and the canopies of rainbows arcing over the site.

Trulzhik Sangyé Önpo Sherab Özer Gyatso
(fourteenth–fifteenth centuries)

In Gyalsé Tulku Drakpa Özer's lineage, Shantipuripa, otherwise known as
the great tertön Trulzhik Sangyé Önpo Sherab Özer Gyatso, appeared as his
principal disciple. Sherab Özer took monastic ordination at the age of seven
and enrolled in the monastic community of Samyé. He received teachings
and empowerments from both the Nyingma and Sarma Schools, and studied under more than fifty masters, including Karmapa Rangjung Dorjé. He
trained in Prajnaparamita, Vinaya, Buddhist logic, and Abhidharma, and
gained recognition as a scholar. Later, when the Omniscient Dharma Lord
Longchenpa was returning from Bhutan and staying at Zhung Mountain,
Trulzhik Sherab Özer met with him. He made many generous offerings to
the guru and the Sangha, and received many empowerments, teachings, and
pointing out instructions in the secret Dzogchen cycles, including both
kama and terma transmissions, as well as transmissions on the Dzogchen
tantra of *The All-Creating Monarch*.

Longchenpa's attendants encouraged him, saying, "You are surely the
lineage successor. You should stay and be the guru's personal secretary." But
with sincere appreciation and affection, Longchenpa advised him, "When
one is young, it may be profitable to study, but this dialectical approach is
for those of little faith. Do not waste your time on it." He gave Trulzhik
Sherab Özer symbols of enlightened body, speech, and mind, as well as his
hat, robes, and sitting mat, and authorized him to pass on the lineage of
ultimate meaning.

Later, when Omniscient Longchenpa was staying at Drikung, Trulzhik
invited him to come to the Chimphu uplands. There Longchenpa bestowed
empowerments and gave teachings from the Nyingthig cycles. After he had
finished teachings on the path of trekchö, Longchenpa passed away. Trulzhik made offerings and honored his guru's remains. He erected both outer
and inner supports, each of which included a shrine. After that he decided
to spend the rest of his life meditating in solitude.

From Tsungmé Ösel Rangdröl he received teachings, empowerments,
and pointing out instructions on the secret Nyingthig cycles. He divided his
time between receiving the teachings from his guru and periods of intensive
practice for six years without interruption.

When Gyalsé Tulku Drakpa Özer was returning from the southern
region of Lhodrak, Trulzhik and his students went to meet him and made

extensive offerings. On several occasions Trulzhik received the complete cycle of teachings from the lineage of Longchenpa, including the two cycles of Vima Nyingthig and Khandro Nyingthig, and did the practices of these cycles as well. His guru, Drakpa Özer, was extremely pleased, and their minds merged, becoming inseparable. Drawing from prophecy, Gyalsé Tulku Drakpa Özer confirmed that Trulzhik was the keeper of his teachings, and Trulzhik viewed the transmissions he received from Gyalsé to be the main source of his lineage.

Trulzhik later devoted himself to practice in remote regions, relying on meager food and shabby clothing, cutting off all involvement with worldly life. Although he had mastered many teachings and empowerments from both the Nyingma and Sarma lineages, he only taught the tradition of the great Longchenpa and only accepted worthy disciples to receive his teachings.

He had many accomplished disciples and entrusted great masters such as Gyalsé Dawa Drakpa and Jatang Drakpa to carry forth his lineage.

Trulzhik spent the latter part of his life at the forest retreat of Palgyi Naktro, located near a spring on the mountain called Riwoché in the region of Drak. He never deviated from his practice or his teaching activities. He passed away amidst amazing signs.

Trulzhik Sherab Özer's principal disciple was Gyalsé Dawa Drakpa, Longchenpa's grandson through Gyalsé Tulku Drakpa Özer.

Gyalsé Dawa Drakpa (fourteenth–fifteenth centuries)

The birth of Gyalsé Dawa Drakpa, which had been prophesied,[8] was at a place called Kalden Jampading in Dra. From a very early age he possessed the qualities of a holy one. By the age of five he knew how to read and write and could recite liturgies with ease. He received the empowerments and transmissions of the Clear Light Great Perfection from his father, along with other Dharma lineage teachings and transmissions.

At the age of twelve he was ordained as a novice monk at Tsetang Shedra. Under the master Gyalsangpa he mastered Buddhist logic and epistemology, Prajnaparamita, Vinaya, Abhidharma, and Shantideva's *Guide to the Bodhisattva's Way of Life*. When he turned eighteen he took full monastic ordination at Tsalmin from the great abbot Sönam Zangpo and was given the name Lodrö Zangpo.

He studied *The Scriptural Transmission of the Vinaya*, the Lojong teachings, the *Six Techniques of Union* from the Kalachakra cycle, and the most secret wrathful form of Hayagriva, as well as many other empowerments. He received a vast range of Dharma teachings from great teachers, and gained a reputation as a superb scholar.

In particular, from Trulzhik Sangyé Önpo he received and mastered, like one vase being filled from another, all the empowerments, teachings, and pith instructions of the tradition of the Omniscient King of the Dharma, his grandfather Longchenpa. Trulzhik named him as his heart son and regent of the ultimate transmission of realization, and entrusted him with the responsibility of continuing the lineage.

He cleared away all his doubts and questions through diligent study and contemplation. By the age of eighteen he had opened the door to the teachings of the Khandro Nyingthig for over two hundred men and women. For many years hence, he taught the two Nyingthig cycles each year without fail, bringing countless students to spiritual maturity and liberation in the Yoru area of Central Tibet.

Later on he followed the footsteps of his father and grandfather south to Bhutan. On his way he stopped at the center founded by Tulku Dorjé Sengé at Kawachen in the region of Lhodrak. There he taught faithful students, including nine important local teachers, according to their capacities. He then spent a year in meditation retreat at the holy lake of Pema Ling.

Continuing on to Bumthang, Ngenlong, Paro, and other places in Bhutan, he gave the people a great sense of faith through his compassionate activities to bring benefit and happiness. He spent three years in retreat in the wilderness of Chöjé Drak and founded the meditation center Samten Ling in Bumthang. His students invited him to Kuré Valley and Dungrang in the east, where he provided an opportunity for them to gather merit. He taught the development of bodhichitta and gave empowerments and teachings according to their wishes. There he was also honored by two rulers from India.

Gyalsé Dawa Drakpa spent long periods practicing intensively in such places as Dza Rinchen Pungpa and Sha-uk Domtsang, focusing unflaggingly on realizing the pinnacle teachings of the Dzogchen Nyingthig. He had visions of the entire array of his personal yidams and experienced the enlightened intent of the Great Perfection—the perception of awareness's naturally manifest appearances without bias—and he attained a high level of realization.

He traveled to Zangyak, Drushül, and other places, where he was received with respect by the terchen Ratna Lingpa, Gönrinpa, and other prominent teachers. He granted the empowerments, teachings, and pith instructions of the Dzogchen approach on a vast scale. He traveled as far as Mao Chokpo in Tamshül, benefiting many students, before returning to Bumthang.

On a number of occasions, many people with the appropriate karma perceived him in the form of Hayagriva. Using his unrestricted psychic power, he foretold events hidden from normal perception, and whenever he taught the Dharma, rainbows appeared, along with many other amazing signs. All of the regions he traveled through or stayed in enjoyed good harvests, an absence of illnesses, and so forth. His boundless Dharma activities brought benefit and happiness to countless students. He thus spent forty years working for the welfare of beings.

Gyalsé Dawa Drakpa finally passed into nirvana on the day of the new moon of the Pig Month in the Rat Year at Samten Ling in Bhutan. After his remains were cremated, many relics, as well as images of deities such as Vajrayogini, were found in the ashes. Throughout Bhutan and the central region of Tibet, memorial services were held to fulfill his last wishes, and outer and inner supports were erected.

And so it was that, continuing on from the master Gyalsé Dawa Drakpa, Omniscient Longchenpa's lineage of the complete cycle of the ripening empowerments and liberating instructions of the Nyingthig, belonging to the Secret Mengagdé Class of Dzogchen, was transmitted in its entirety through the unbroken stream of successive lineage holders as follows:

- ▸ Drupchen Künzang Dorjé (fourteenth–fifteenth centuries)
- ▸ Chöjé Kunga Gyaltsen Pelzang (1497–1568)
- ▸ Tulku Natsok Rangdröl (1494–1571)
- ▸ Tulku Tenzin Drakpa (1536–1597)
- ▸ Khedrup Dongak Tenzin (1576–1628)
- ▸ Rigdzin Chenpo Trinlé Lhündrup (1611–1662)
- ▸ Terdak Lingpa (Terchen Gyurmé Dorjé) (1646–1714)
- ▸ Gyalsé Rinchen Namgyal (1694–1758)
- ▸ Ngak Rabjampa Orgyen Chödrak (1676–?)
- ▸ Ngakyi Rabjampa Orgyen Palgön (Drupwang Shrinatha) (eighteenth century)
- ▸ Rigdzin Jigmé Lingpa (1730–1798)

Rigdzin Jigmé Lingpa

One cannot conclude the story of Longchenpa without emphasizing the Omniscient Knowledge Holder Jigmé Lingpa. As one of the central figures in the propagation of the Nyingthig teachings, Jigmé Lingpa's life story is presented extensively in other works, so only a brief excerpt of his story is included here.

RIGDZIN JIGMÉ LINGPA

Jigmé Lingpa appeared as the incarnation of both Vimalamitra and King Trisong Detsen. His coming into this world was foretold by Guru Rinpoché over eight hundred years before his birth:

> In the south there will be a tulku named Özer.
> He will liberate beings through the profound teachings of
> Nyingthig.
> He will lead to the pure land of the knowledge holders whoever is
> connected to him.

From a young age Jigmé Lingpa demonstrated an unusually intense passion for the Dharma; he felt uncontrived devotion to Guru Rinpoché, and he had innate compassion for all living beings, especially animals. And so all this imbued his childhood with great joyfulness and deep meaningfulness. In addition, he had extraordinary devotion toward Omniscient Longchenpa.

At the beginning of his twenty-eighth year he began a three-year retreat at Palri Monastery. During this time he read Longchenpa's Seven Treasuries, and through his study of those sublime works he was able to resolve all his questions regarding his meditative experiences.

In that same year, while in a state of intense devotion to Guru Rinpoché, he entered a deep meditative experience of clear light. While absorbed in that state he had the experience of riding a white lion while flying through the sky. After a while he reached the circumambulation path of Jarungkhasor, the Great Stupa at Boudanath in Nepal.

In the eastern courtyard he saw a wisdom dakini as a dharmakaya appearance. She gave him a beautiful wooden casket, saying,

> For pure minded disciples
> You are Trisong Detsen.
> For disciples with impure mind
> You are Sengé Repa.
> This is the mind treasure of Samantabhadra,
> The symbolic scripts of Padmasambhava, the knowledge holder, and
> The great secret treasures of the dakinis. Signs are over!

After speaking thusly the dakini disappeared. He then opened the casket and within it he found five rolls of yellow scrolls and seven crystal beads. Among these were the teachings of the Longchen Nyingthig cycle, The Heart Essence of the Vast Expanse. Encouraged by another dakini, Jigmé Lingpa then swallowed all the yellow scrolls and the crystal beads. Upon doing so he immediately experienced all the words of the Longchen Nyingthig along with their meaning awaken in his mind as a terma, as if they were imprinted there. After he came out of that experience, he remained in the realization of rigpa, intrinsic awareness, the union of bliss and emptiness.

After this revelation he kept the Longchen Nyingthig teachings and empowerments secret for seven years so that he, as the treasure revealer, could practice the teachings himself before revealing them.

At the age of thirty-one he began a second three-year retreat at Samyé Chimphu. During this retreat he awakened to the highest realization of

Dzogpa Chenpo through three pure visions of the wisdom body of Long-chenpa. In the first vision he received the blessing of the vajra body of Long-chenpa and obtained the transmission of both the words and meaning of Longchenpa's teachings. In the second vision he received the speech bless-ing of Longchenpa, which authorized him to spread the profound teach-ings of Longchenpa as his representative. In the third vision Jigmé Lingpa received the blessing of the wisdom mind of Longchenpa, which transferred the sublime power of Longchenpa's enlightened intrinsic awareness to him directly. He also entrusted Jigmé Lingpa with a book and told him, "All the esoteric instructions that are concealed in *The Great Chariot* and in my other works are clarified herein." Longchenpa also told him, "May realiza-tion of the meaning be transferred to you and may the transmission of the words be completely accomplished."

When Longchenpa had transmitted all the instructions and further advice to him, Jigmé Lingpa came to comprehend thoroughly the oceanic doctrine, and all the textual traditions and instructions of the Omniscient Longchenpa in particular. After this, all became naturally free and open in oneness.

Following this awakening, he composed *Künkhyen Zhalung* and other writings as the true meaning of Longchenpa's Seven Treasuries.

It is said that Jigmé Lingpa's mind treasure revelations are called the *Longchen Nyingthig* for three reasons. First, they are the innermost heart essence (*nyingthig*) teachings received by him through the blessing of the three pure visions he had of Omniscient Longchen Rabjam. Secondly, they are the condensation and essence of all the Nyingthig teachings that came through Longchenpa. Thirdly, they are the "heart essence" (or *nyingthig*) teachings on *longchen*, the "vast expanse," the highest teachings of Bud-dhism. Thus it is sometimes translated into English as meaning "The Heart Essence of Longchenpa."

Jigmé Lingpa was an incarnation of both Vimalamitra and King Trisong Detsen, who in turn received the Nyingthig teachings from both Guru Rinpoché and Vimalamitra. And so, the Nyingthig teachings of the two lineages were merged together in Jigmé Lingpa. The Longchen Nyingthig is thus the essence of the two Nyingthig traditions, the Khandro Nyingthig and the Vima Nyingthig. The two traditions of the Khandro Nyingthig and the Vima Nyingthig have become known as the Early Nyingthig, and the tradition of the Longchen Nyingthig as the Later Nyingthig.

Because of its simplicity, clarity, and power, the Longchen Nyingthig tradition of Jigmé Lingpa has become the most popular transmission of Dzogchen Nyingthig teachings in recent times; countless streams of this transmission continue to benefit beings throughout the world today. Practically all of the renowned and great teachers of the day, from all over Tibet and its surroundings, came to receive teachings at his feet. In this way Jigmé Lingpa firmly established the Dzogchen teachings for the benefit of those in his time and those in the future as well.

Under Jigmé Lingpa's careful supervision the royal family of Dergé, and especially Queen Tsewang Lhamo, who became one of his main patrons, paid for the publication of his collected works, in addition to his compiled collection called Collected Tantras of the Nyingma School. As a result of their vast efforts to preserve and spread the Nyingma lineage, Longchenpa and Jigmé Lingpa came to be referred to as "the omniscient father and son."

Shortly after attaining his seventieth year, having fully transmitted all his teachings, Rigdzin Jigmé Lingpa moved to Namdröl Tsé, the new upper hermitage at Tsering Jong. The next day, the third day of the ninth month of the Earth Horse Year (1798), he gave a White Tara teaching. From the early morning on the air of the entire hermitage was filled with a strong and pleasant fragrance. A gentle rain sprinkled unceasingly from the blue and cloudless sky, and there was not even the slightest trace of wind. In the early evening he requested that new offerings be set on the altar. Then he sat himself in the *rishi* posture and merged his awareness into the primordial nature.

Jigmé Lingpa was also known as Khyentsé Özer (Rays of Wisdom and Compassion). His rebirth appeared as five different tulku manifestations: Jamyang Khyentsé Wangpo (1820–1892) was his body emanation; the amazing Patrul Rinpoché (1808–1887) was his speech emanation; Do Khyentsé Yeshé Dorjé (1800–1866) was his mind emanation; Mingyur Namkhai Dorjé (1793–1870), the Fourth Dzogchen Rinpoché, was his enlightened qualities manifestation; and Gyalsé Shenpen Tayé (1800–1870) was his enlightened activities manifestation.[9]

The Lineage from Jigmé Lingpa to the Present Day

Among Jigmé Lingpa's countless disciples, two of his foremost heart sons were Jigmé Gyalwé Nyugu (1765–1823) and the First Dodrupchen, Jigmé Trinlé Özer (1745–1821). These two carried forth the Clear Light Great Perfection teachings as an ever-increasing stream flowing down to us even to this present day.

Entrance to Longchenpa's cave at Samyé Chimphu.

Longchenpa's meditation seat at Tharpa Ling in Bhutan.

VIEW FROM LONGCHENPA'S MEDITATION SEAT AT THARPA LING IN BHUTAN.

LONGCHENPA'S RELIQUARY STUPA AT SAMYÉ CHIMPHU.

Through the great Jigmé Gyalwé Nyugu, his first heart son, the renowned Dza Patrul Rinpoché, author of *The Words of My Perfect Teacher,* received the complete transmission and passed this lineage on to Nyoshul Lungtok Tenpai Nyima (1829–1912), who transmitted it to Khenpo Ngagchung[10] (1879–1941), who passed it on to Lungtrul Shedrup Tenpai Nyima (1920–?), to the Second Drubwang Pema Norbu, Rigdzin Palchen Dupa (1887–1932), to Choktrul Chökyi Dawa (1894–1959), to the Third Drupwang Pema Norbu, Jigmé Thubten Shedrup Chökyi Drayang (Kyabjé Penor Rinpoché) (1932–2009), an emanation of Vimalamitra and guru of many masters in our present day. Each of these gurus nurtured many realized disciples, and each has a wondrous story of inspiration that one can find told beautifully elsewhere.

The second heart son of Jigmé Gyalwé Nyugu was the peerless Jamyang Khyentsé Wangpo (1820–1892), the tulku of Rigdzin Jigmé Lingpa and one of the main founders of the Rimé (nonsectarian) movement. Many great stories are told of his life events. One of his eminent heart sons was Dza Pukhung Gyurmé Ngedon Wangpo (nineteenth–twentieth centuries), from whom Dudjom Rinpoché Jigdral Yeshé Dorjé (1904–1987) received the transmission lineage. Dudjom Rinpoché's two sons, Thinley Norbu (1931–2011) and Shenpa Dawa (1950–present), along with his many realized living disciples, have spread the Dharma of the Dzogchen Nyingthig throughout the seven continents of our present-day world.

Another famous heart son of Jamyang Khyentsé Wangpo was the great Adzom Drukpa Rinpoché, Drodul Pawo Dorjé (1842–1924). Adzom Drukpa was reborn as two tulkus: Druktrul Rinpoché (twentieth century) and Chögyal Namkhai Norbu Rinpoché (1938–present), the latter living master being his mind emanation.

It was Adzom Drukpa who transmitted the lineage to Jamyang Khyentsé Chökyi Lodrö[11] (1893–1959), the activity emanation of Jamyang Khyentsé Wangpo. Jamyang Khyentsé Chökyi Lodrö was the main teacher of Kyabjé Dilgo Khyentsé Rinpoché (1910–1991), who was the mind emanation of Jamyang Khyentsé Wangpo and was also the main teacher of Sogyal Rinpoché (1947–present). Dilgo Khyentsé Rinpoché taught countless disciples and lineage holders who are still living, including His Holiness Tenzin Gyatso, the Fourteenth Dalai Lama.

From Rigdzin Jigmé Lingpa's other main disciple, the First Dodrupchen, came such renowned lineage holders as Shabkar Tsokdruk Rangdröl (1781–

1851), author of *The Flight of the Garuda* and *The Life of Shabkar*; and the great female adept Shuksep Lochen Chönyi Zangmo (1865–1953), who was one of Khetsun Sangpo Rinpoché's (1920–2009) main gurus. The Dodrupchen lineage continues to this day.

Indeed there have sprung so many realized masters in the unbroken Dzogchen lineage, from Longchenpa to Pema Lingpa and Jigmé Lingpa down to our present living teachers. Thus the Heart Essence teachings have been kept vital and alive through those who realized the teachings by receiving the precious transmission and by their own diligent practice for the benefit of all sentient beings.

LONGCHENPA'S WRITTEN WORKS

Longchenpa thoroughly studied every one of the many Buddhist vehicles and lineages of teachings in existence in Tibet at the time. Through his radiant intellect, in both his teachings and written works he was able to masterfully reconcile the seeming discrepancies and contradictions between the various presentations of the view and the path within the many lineages of transmission. His written works are also known for being able to transfer true blessings just by reading or hearing his enlightened words.

He wrote teaching manuals for each of these traditions, but most of these have been lost. Some were reclaimed by the dakas and dakinis. Many of his original drafts were lost before they could be published in block print form when a pack animal bearing them stumbled while crossing a deep abyss in Central Bhutan, sending the texts plummeting into the ravine below, never to be found. Others of his works were lost in the vast destruction of temples and libraries after 1959 under the Communist Chinese rule.

Altogether, according to his own index, *The Treasure Chamber*, Longchen Rabjam composed 307 works that remained in the human realm.[12] These works covered not only the entire range of Dharma, and in particular Dzogpa Chenpo, but also such secular subjects as poetry, plays, literature, Sanskrit grammar, metrics, weights and measures, semantics, and literary composition.

Some of his surviving major scholarly and sacred works are:

A. The Seven Great Treasuries (Dzöchen Dün)

1. *The Precious Treasury of Wish Fulfillment* (*Yizhin Rinpoché Dzö*) is written in twenty-two chapters and includes its autocommentary,

White Lotus (*Pema Karpo*), with associated treatises. It presents a survey of the whole range of Mahayana Buddhist doctrine, elucidating the ways of study, analysis, and training in Mahayana and Vajrayana.

2. *The Precious Treasury of Pith Instructions* (*Mengag Rinpoché Dzö*) is a treatise that uses various series of six parts to summarize the Buddhist sutras and tantras, particularly the essence of the path and result in the full scope of Dzogchen and its ethical, philosophical, and meditative instructions. This work, beautifully created in the form of poetic verse, was classified by Longchenpa as "path with result," or *Lamdré*.

3. *The Precious Treasury of the Basic Space of Phenomena*[13] (*Chöying Rinpoché Dzö*) is a brief yet eloquent song in thirteen chapters along with its autocommentary, *A Treasure Trove of Scriptural Transmission* (*Lungki Ter Dzö*). This is an exposition of the profound and vast teachings of ground, path, and result of the three main categories of Dzogpa Chenpo, namely Semdé, Longdé, and Mengagdé, and in particular Longdé.

4. *The Precious Treasury of Philosophical Systems* (*Drupta Rinpoché Dzö*) in eight chapters is a presentation of the various philosophical tenets of all the yanas of sutric and tantric Buddhism, as well as of non-Buddhist systems.

5. *The Precious Treasury of the Supreme Vehicle* (*Thegchog Rinpoché Dzö*) in twenty-five chapters is an eloquent and profound treatise which thoroughly elucidates a meaning commentary of the Seventeen Tantras and One Hundred and Nineteen Instructional Treatises of Mengagdé. It expounds a wide range of Buddhist doctrine, from the manifestation of the absolute teacher as the three kayas to the achievement of the spontaneously accomplished final result of Dzogchen practice, emphasizing tögal in particular. Longchenpa is said to have written this text to fulfill the aspirations of his master Rigdzin Kumaradza at the time of his teacher's death.

6. *The Precious Treasury of Words and Meanings* (*Tshigdön Rinpoché Dzö*). This amazing work is a summary of *The Precious Treasury of the Supreme Vehicle* in eleven chapters, explaining the eleven crucial points, or vajra topics, of tögal practice, in reliance upon the scriptural authority of the Seventeen Tantras. It begins with a description of the ground, clarifies the key points of the path, and concludes with the result, the state of ultimate liberation.

7. *The Precious Treasury of the Natural State*[14] (*Nelug Rinpoché Dzö*). Presented in five chapters (with its autocommentary, *The Exposition of the Quintessential Meaning of the Three Categories*), it explains the ultimate meaning of all three divisions of Dzogpa Chenpo.

B. *The Trilogy of Finding Comfort and Ease (Ngalso Korsum)*[15]

The Three Cycles of Finding Comfort and Ease consist of three root texts, three summaries, called "garlands," three autocommentaries, called "chariots," and three "meaning commentaries" (or instructions on practice), totaling fifteen treatises in all:

1. *Finding Comfort and Ease in the Nature of Mind (Semnyi Ngalso)*, the root text in thirteen chapters; its summary (lost); an autocommentary on the root text; a summary of the autocommentary; and the instructions on practice. The *Semnyi Ngalso* explains all the stages of the view, the ground, path, and the beginning, middle, and end of the sutric and tantric teachings.

2. *Finding Comfort and Ease in Meditation (Samten Ngalso)* consists of the root text in three chapters; its summary; its autocommentary; and the instructions on practice. The text is an instruction on the profound path of achieving meditative stability, resting in self-existent natural wisdom, and presents many practice methods for its attainment. It also includes instructions for finding the ideal outer environment for retreat practice, based on both general considerations and the temperament and constitution of the individual yogi.

3. *Finding Comfort and Ease in the Illusoriness of Things (Gyuma Ngalso)* consists of the root text in eight chapters; its summary; an autocommentary; and the instruction on practice. This text is an instruction on how to view the illusoriness of all appearances, and on cutting the ties of attachment to phenomenal existence through the teachings on eight illusory examples.

There are two additional texts: a summary of The Three Cycles on Finding Comfort and Ease entitled *The Well-Explained Ocean (Legshé Gyatso)* and a table of contents called *Pema Tongden*. The three autocommentaries on The Three Cycles on Finding Comfort and Ease are also known as The Three Chariots (*Shingta Namsum*).

C. *The Trilogy of Natural Freedom (Rangdröl Korsum)*

The Trilogy of Natural Freedom are the "meaning commentaries" on the instructions of the Semdé Class of Dzogpa Chenpo teachings:

1. *The Natural Freedom of Mind Itself (Semnyi Rangdröl)* in three chapters, and a meaning commentary or instruction on practice entitled *Heart Essence of the Stages of the Path (Lamrim Nyingpo)*.
2. *The Natural Freedom of Dharmata (Chönyi Rangdröl)* in three chapters, and an instruction on practice entitled *Precious Jewel Heart Essence (Rinchen Nyingpo)*.
3. *The Natural Freedom of Equality (Nyamnyi Rangdröl)* in three chapters, and an instruction on practice entitled *The Wish-fulfilling Heart Essence (Yizhin Nyingpo)*.

D. *The Three Innermost Essences (Yangthig Namsum)*

These texts contain the crucial points of the esoteric oral teachings of Mengagdé, the highest of the three divisions of Dzogpa Chenpo. In these texts special emphasis is placed on tögal training. They are included within his compilation of the *Four Branches of the Heart Essence (Nyingthig Yabzhi)* along with the Khandro Nyingthig and the Vima Nyingthig.

1. The Innermost Essence of the Lama (*Lama Yangthig*) or The Very Profound Vision of the Wish-fulfilling Gem (*Yangzab Yizhin Norbu*) consists of thirty-five treatises commenting on the Vima Nyingthig. It condenses and interprets the vast material of The Four Volumes of Esoteric Teachings of Vima Nyingthig and One Hundred and Nineteen Treatises of Instruction of Mengagdé of Dzogpa Chenpo. The Four Volumes of Esoteric Teachings are: *The Great Golden Letters (Seryig Chen)*, *The Great Turquoise Letters (Yuyig Chen)*, *The Great Conch-colored Letters (Düngyig)*, *The Great Copper Letters (Zangyig Chen)*, and *The Great Variegated Jewel Inlaid Letters (Trayig Chen)*.
2. The Innermost Essence of the Dakini (*Khandro Yangthig*) consists of fifty-five treatises. In Longchen Rabjam's previous life as Pema Ledrel Tsal he had authority over the texts of the Khandro Nyingthig. In his life as Longchenpa he again received the transmissions

of the ripening empowerments and liberating instructions and gained realization of the Khandro Nyingthig teachings. He then wrote the texts entitled Khandro Yangthig, elaborating on the Khandro Nyingthig. In its seventy-three chapters he defines the three sections of pith instructions from the Khandro Nyingthig, which are: the practical instructions on the essence of the transmission based on the dakini's prophecies; instructions on how to present the empowerments and teachings; and advice on the heart essence of definitive meaning, which causes blessings to arise in one's mind.

3. *The Profound Innermost Essence* (*Zabmo Yangthig*) is the most detailed and profound commentary on both the Vima Nyingthig and the Khandro Nyingthig.

E. Three Cycles on Dispelling the Darkness (Münsel Korsum)

These three texts are commentaries on the *Guhyagarbha Tantra* according to the Nyingthig view:

1. *Dispelling the Darkness of the Mind* (*Chidön Yikyi Münsel*), an overview of the general meaning;
2. *Dispelling the Darkness of Ignorance* (*Dudön Marig Münsel*), a synopsis of the essential meaning;
3. *Dispelling Darkness in the Ten Directions* (*Drelwa Chogchu Münsel*), a major commentary.

HIS VARIOUS NAMES

In the Tibetan Buddhist tradition one is given different names upon receiving ordinations (such as the Pratimoksha vows of monastic and lay ordination, Refuge vows, and Bodhisattva vows) and tantric empowerments. In addition, names may be granted as titles to ones of great accomplishment.

Longchen Rabjam signed his vast body of written works using his different names and their meanings to designate the different categories or levels of his work. Thus, by knowing how he signed his work, one can determine the class of teachings he is presenting in any given text.

▶ In his writings that teach the expanse of inconceivable nature in greatest detail, he signed "by Longchen Rabjam (Infinite Great Vast

Expanse)" or "Longchen Rabjampa (Possessor of the Infinite Great Vast Expanse [of Knowledge])," i.e., the name conferred upon him while he was still a young scholar monk at Sangphu (or, alternately, said to have been bestowed upon him by King Tai Situ Changchub Gyaltsen on his return from Bhutan, after they were reconciled).

► In his writings that are mainly on interpretable subjects, including the mundane studies such as poetry, metrics, and the science of words (language), he signed "by Samyepa Tsultrim Lodrö (the Disciplined and Intelligent Man from Samyé)," his monastic ordination name.

► In his writings that relate to both outer and inner tantras, he signed "by Dorjé Ziji (Vajra Brilliance)," the name given to him by Khandro Yeshé Tsogyal.[16]

► In his writings that are mainly on profound subjects explained through the stages of the yanas, and on the words and meaning which explain the stages of contemplations, he signed "by Drimé Özer (Stainless Light Rays)," the name given to him by Guru Padmakara.[17]

► In his writings in which the yanas, theories, suchness, and so forth are explained in detail, he signed "by Künkhyen Ngagi Wangpo (Omniscient Lord of Speech)."

Other names by which Longchenpa is known include:

► Künkhyen Chöjé (Omniscient Dharma Lord)
► Penpa Zangpo (Noble Benefactor)
► Pema Ledrel Tsal (Lotus of Dynamic Karmic Connections)
► Namkhai Naljor (Space Yogi)
► Natsok Rangdröl (Natural Freedom of the Myriad Display)
► Guyang Lodé (Spacious Mind of Bliss)
► Lodrö Chokden (Possessed of Sublime Intelligence)
► Longsel Drimé (Immaculate Lucid Expanse)
► Samyé Lungmangpa (Samyé's Recipient of Many Transmissions)

And so this story of the life and legacy of the Omniscient Dharma Lord Longchen Rabjam draws to a close. Please know that words cannot begin to describe the magnificence of this incomparable man, nor can they convey the vast and inconceivable extent of how he has helped beings, throughout his life, his former lives, and his subsequent lives, through his example, his attainment, his oral teachings, his written works, and through his disciples and lineage holders who carried on his teachings and transmissions through their own study, practice, and realization. He is like a great father torch, from whom many other torches have been lit, clearing away the darkness of ignorance, bringing the light of knowledge and the warmth of experience and realization, and spreading joy and peace to countless beings throughout time and space.

Here are Longchenpa's simple parting words of personal advice for us: "My future followers! Leave your worldly activities of this life behind. Begin your preparations for your next lives. Rely on a perfect and virtuous teacher. Receive instructions on the essence of clear light. Practice the secret teachings of Nyingthig in solitude. Transcend samsara and nirvana in this very lifetime!"[18]

In Praise of Longchen Rabjam

by Khenpo Shenga

Translated by Adam Pearcey

D UE TO THE kindness of Guru Padmasambhava, there have been many
great holders of the teachings here in Tibet, the Land of Snows. There
have appeared highly accomplished saints who were no different from the
vidyadharas of India, the Land of the Aryas. Yet although there have been
countless eminent scholars, none of them might be compared with the
Six Ornaments and Two Supreme Ones of India[1] in terms of wisdom and
enlightened activity.

In later times there was the Omniscient One from Samyé, Longchenpa,
who was the equal of the Jowo Kadampa geshés in terms of his ethical discipline and practice of training the mind (lojong), and who was like Jetsun
Milarepa in how he first served his teacher and then spent his life meditating in solitude on the guru's instructions. On account of his total mastery
of study and contemplation, his fearless eloquence and his achievements in
explanation, debate, and composition, we might compare him to the likes
of Sakya Pandita, the Lord of Dharma, or the precious Je Tsongkhapa. How
he reached the final accomplishment and arrived at the exhaustion of reality
within the primordial state was just like the great Chetsun Sengé Wangchuk,
Melong Dorjé, and others. In terms of his ability to manipulate phenomenal
existence and call upon the assistance of the oath-bound guardians, he was
comparable to the great awareness holders of Nub. In keeping to the tenets
of the pinnacle of all yanas and surpassing all the views and philosophies fab-
ricated by the ordinary mind, he was like the great Rongzom. If we consider
the vast array of instructions he passed on in an oral lineage and the way he
cared for the disciples who maintained his tradition, we might compare him
to Sachen Kunga Nyingpo or Marpa Lotsawa.

His mastery over the conventional sciences and the way in which Sarasvati, the goddess of learning, lent power to his speech[2] made him the equal of the lotsawas[3] of the past. The way great clouds of blessings are amassed within his written instructions makes them identical to the profound Dharma treasures of the great tertöns. His perfect training in bodhichitta and his ability to benefit all those with whom he came into contact was reminiscent of Dromtonpa or the peerless Dakpo Lhajé (Gampopa).

Other Tibetan scholars took as their basis the excellent Indian treatises but then added explanations based on their own clever ideas, with the result that on occasion their statements no longer accord with scripture or valid reasoning. In particular, the works of Nagarjuna and his successors have been fervently debated among Tibetans, with the assertions of earlier Tibetan scholars subjected to a great deal of presumptuous refutation and affirmation by later scholars. Yet the explanations of the Omniscient One remain true to the tradition of the Six Ornaments and Two Supreme Ones in their beginning, middle, and end.

Other Tibetan siddhas possessed only a few instructions from the oral lineage and then taught the holders of their tradition to meditate on selected instructions. Gyalwa Longchenpa, by contrast, was the master of countless teachings from profound transmissions. He possessed all manner of instructions, which had been passed down from vidyadharas and accomplished siddhas, from dakas and dakinis, or received directly from Guru Padmasambhava and so on. This meant he could lead the holders of his tradition to attainment by encouraging them to practice diligently those instructions for which they felt the greatest affinity.

Other learned and accomplished masters may have given complete teachings on particular instructions, but they did not have practices for all the teachings in their entirety. The Omniscient Guru explained all the teachings completely. He revealed the instructions for gaining supreme and common accomplishments in general, from the kriya- and charyatantras onwards, and all the tantras and pith instructions of Dzogpa Chenpo in particular, and so he is the true charioteer of the essence of clear light teachings.[4]

In addition, his wisdom body has appeared in visions before those with great good fortune, granting them realization and so on.[5]

In short, I believe Gyalwa Longchenpa to be the unique embodiment of the enlightened qualities of all the learned and accomplished masters of the Land of Snows. If you consider this honestly, you will find this to be just how it is, neither an exaggeration nor an understatement.

Gaining experience and realization through meditation—
That is common to all forms of pith instruction.
But gaining experience and realization through nonmeditation—
How could anyone fail to seize upon something so amazing?

Ha! Ha!

So did the omniscient master reveal in his sublime works
The entire range of the Victorious One's teachings.
Never before had any of the wise masters of India or Tibet
Left such a legacy to the world.

—Patrul Rinpoché (1808–1887)*

* Translated in *Mind in Comfort and Ease*, p. xix.

Notes

Preface

1. From a teaching on Longchenpa's *Samten Ngalso* (*Resting at Ease in Meditative Stability*) given in Crestone, Colorado in April, 2010; translated by Erik Drew.
2. From an oral teaching on Longchenpa's *Semnyi Ngalso* given in Pinehurst, Texas; translated by Anne C. Klein.
3. Nyoshul Khenpo, *A Marvelous Garland of Rare Gems: Biographies of Masters of Awareness in the Dzogchen Lineage*, p. xxxii.
4. David Francis Germano, "Poetic Thought, the Intelligent Universe, and the Mystery of Self: The Tantric Synthesis of rDzogs Chen in Fourteenth Century Tibet" (Ph.D. diss., University of Wisconsin, 1992), p. 3.
5. *Heart Essence of the Dakinis.*

Introduction

1. Also spelled Vairotsana.
2. Cannibals said to dwell in a magical realm. Guru Rinpoché went there to convert the cannibals and to prevent them from invading the human realm. Sometimes called *rakshasas*, or *monpa*.
3. Lhacham is a title of royalty, in this case indicating her status as a princess.
4. *Atiyoga* is one of the Sanskrit terms for Dzogchen; another term is *Mahasandhi*.
5. This famous mountain is known in China as Wu Tai Shan. Legend has it that Vimalamitra is still alive on Wu Tai Shan due to his accomplishment of the deathless Great Transference Body, and appears to worthy practitioners. It's said that Manjushri dwells there as well.
6. The three realms of cyclic existence are the Desire Realm, the Form Realm, and the Formless Realm.

Prelude

1. Keith Dowman, trans., *The Legend of the Great Stupa and The Life Story of the Lotus Born* (Berkeley: Tibetan Nyingma Meditation Center, 1973), pp. 21–38.

2. *Lama Yang Sang Thug Kyi Drub.*
3. The name of the Great Stupa, Jarungkhasor, combines the words *jarung*—meaning "work," and *khasor*—meaning "permission."

CHAPTER ONE: HIS PREVIOUS LIVES

1. See Glossary: the six extraordinary qualities of Samantabhadra.
2. For a detailed account of this transmission, see Erik Pema Kunsang, *Wellsprings of the Great Perfection,* pp. 157–160.
3. Although one hundred thousand dakinis were present, these three were the only human disciples to receive the Khandro Nyingthig at that time, according to Gangteng Tulku Rinpoché.
4. Mendicants, yogis, and yoginis who focus more on meditation practice than on the scholarly pandita style of learning to reveal the inner meaning.
5. According to Nyoshul Khenpo and Richard Barron (Chökyi Nyima), this "seal" is a metaphor for the decisiveness in giving the entrustment, involving formally investing the student with the responsibility to serve as the next lineage holder of that teaching. (Nyoshul Khenpo, *A Marvelous Garland of Rare Gems,* p. 627, n. 65)
6. Chimphu is the mountain overlooking Samyé Monastery, the first monastery in Tibet, established by King Trisong Detsen, Guru Rinpoché Padmasambhava, and Shantarakshita. Many retreat caves are on the mountain, including caves used by Longchenpa for mountain retreat. Even today, many yogis and yoginis are using these caves for meditation retreat.
7. Other accounts give Princess Pemasal's age as fifteen at the time.
8. The Union of Samantabhadra's Intent (*Künzang Gongdu*) is a complete Dzogchen cycle of the Mengagdé or pith instruction Nyingthig class. Along with Lama Jewel Ocean (*Lama Norbu Gyatso*) and The Great Compassionate One: The Lamp That Dispels the Darkness (*Thugjé Chenpo Münsel Dronmé*), this was one of the three principal termas later discovered by the tertön King Pema Lingpa, Princess Pemasal's next major incarnation following her rebirth as Longchenpa.
9. *Lama Norbu Gyatso,* a guru yoga of the eight manifestations of Padmasambhava.
10. *Thugjé Chenpo Münsel Dronmé,* a profound two-armed yab-yum Red Chenrezig terma cycle embracing the pinnacle view within the Great Perfection.
11. *Sengé Naring Drak.*
12. It was Longchenpa's prior incarnation, Pema Ledrel Tsal, who actually revealed the Khandro Nyingthig and the kusali cycle, and his subsequent incarnation as Pema Lingpa who revealed the Learned Pandita cycle of terma treasures. It was through Longchenpa that the Khandro Nyingthig truly spread and was brought to fullness within Longchenpa's combined cycle of the Nyingthig Yabzhi.
13. The great treasure finder (tertön) Nyang Nyima Özer was the first of the "five tertön kings."
14. Guru Chökyi Wangchuk (1212–1273) was the second of the "five tertön kings."

Together with Nyang Nyima Özer they were known as "the sun and moon," and their termas were known as the Upper and Lower Termas.

15. Orgyen Lingpa (1323–1360) was a revealer of many terma treasures and lived in the same region as Ngakchang Rinchen Drakpa.

16. *Dzogchen Pema Nyingthig.*

17. Tsuldor is short for Tsultrim Dorjé.

18. Sungtrul Rinpoché writes that the termas were found in the same area, but extracted from near the north side of a single-trunk juniper tree, rather than from a cave. (See Sarah Harding, *The Life and Revelations of Pema Lingpa,* p. 32)

19. Homemade Tibetan barley beer.

20. The Third Karmapa, whose later Dzogchen transmission became known as the *Karma Nyingthig.*

21. "An almost mythical substance known as the 'flesh of a Brahmin born seven times' (*dromtsé*). It means the flesh of one who has been consecutively reborn as a Brahmin for seven lifetimes through one's accumulated store of merit, and is thus imbued with special magical properties. This substance, mentioned in ancient Indian and Tibetan treatises, when eaten, can propel even the most ordinary person into a direct experience of the nature of mind. This is called 'liberation through taste.' The dromtsé, often concealed as terma, is sometimes combined with more than seventy herbs and flowers, a number of which are discovered as terma themselves, and made into pills (*rilbu*). A long and involved ritual procedure follows to make and consecrate the pills."—Joseph Wagner, private communication.

22. The dakini Vajrayogini.

23. Rinchen Lingpa (1295–1375) was one of the "Eight Lingpas," famous treasure revealers of the Nyingma School.

24. This spot is known as Phabong Rubal Nakpo (Black Turtle Boulder). (Sarah Harding, *The Life and Revelations of Pema Lingpa,* p. 33)

25. *Dharmadhatu,* the basic space of phenomena.

CHAPTER TWO: HIS BIRTH AND EARLY LIFE

1. The first conqueror, or buddha, in this context was probably Vimalamitra, the author of the Vima Nyingthig. It could also refer to Padmasambhava (Guru Rinpoché), who taught Dzogchen extensively in Tibet. In *A Marvelous Garden of Precious Gems,* p. 631, n. 3, it is said to refer to Buddha Shakyamuni, the historical buddha of our era.

2. The three categories of Dzogchen teachings are the Mind Class of teachings (*Semdé*), the Space Class of teachings (*Longdé*), and the Oral Pith Instruction Class of teachings (*Mengagdé*).

3. Nyoshul Khenpo gives the village name as Entsa in *A Marvelous Garden of Precious Gems,* p. 98.

4. According to Dudjom Rinpoche's *The Nyingma School of Tibetan Buddhism,* vol. 1, p. 575, Öki Kyinkorchen was the ruler of Ngenlam. Gyalwa Chokyang was one

of Guru Rinpoché's twenty-five closest disciples. He was an accomplished master of the practice of the deity Hayagriva, and one of the first seven Tibetans chosen to receive monastic ordination, also called the "seven probationers" or "seven men who were tested." Abbot Shantarakshita ordained these seven initially as a test to see if Tibetans could uphold the monastic vows. Evidently they passed the test!

5. In *A Marvelous Garland of Rare Gems*, p. 98, Nyoshul Khenpo states that Lhasung lived to the age of 105, not 150. However, in *The Nyingma School of Tibetan Buddhism*, vol. 1, p. 575, Dudjom Rinpoché gives the age of 150, which would be more noteworthy as a sign of alchemical accomplishment.

6. Dromtönpa (1004–1064) was one of the three leading personal disciples of Jowo Atisha and a founder of the Kadampa order.

7. In *The Practice of Dzogchen*, p. 146, Tulku Thondup states that Longchenpa was eleven when his father died.

8. "Disciplined Intellect." Here "intellect" means that all objects of knowledge can be easily understood without limitation, indicating someone who can teach and write with utter clarity through sounds and words.

CHAPTER THREE: HIS EARLY TEACHERS AND TRAINING

1. Lamdré means "fruit and path."

2. The Medicine Buddha.

3. Pacification (Shijé or zhi byed) of suffering, one of the eight main traditions of Tibetan Buddhism founded by Padampa Sangyé, a siddha who visited Tibet several times in the twelfth century, based on the principles of Prajnaparamita.

4. Also called Sangphu Neuthang. Founded by Ngok Lekpé Sherab, a direct student of the great Atisha, Sangphu was the greatest academy in Tibet for the study of Buddhist logic. It was the most important learning center in the country at the time of Longchenpa.

5. Tsengönpa was the fifteenth to hold the seat of Lingo at Sangphu.

6. Labrangpa Chöpal Gyaltsen was the sixteenth to hold the seat of Lingo at Sangphu.

7. The *Samadhiraja Sutra*.

8. The name Longchenpa is the shortened form of Longchen Rabjampa.

9. On page 117 in *A Marvelous Garland of Rare Gems*, Nyoshul Khenpo's account says that it was Tai Situ who conferred this title upon Longchenpa. However, both Tulku Thondup's account in *Masters of Meditation and Miracles* and Dudjom Rinpoché's account in *The Nyingma School of Tibetan Buddhism* say that it was while still a young scholar at Sangphu that he was given this name by which we know him today.

10. Although no name is given at this point, his preceptors were previously named as Samdrup Rinchen of Samyé and Lopön Kunga Özer, from whom he received his novice monk ordination.

11. Dudjom Rinpoché gives the deity name of Yamari instead of Yamantaka here. (See Dudjom Rinpoche, *The Nyingma School of Tibetan Buddhism*, vol. 1, p. 578)

12. A disciple in the line of the three famous gurus of the lineage of Pacification, namely Ma (Chökyi Sherab), So(-chung Gedünbar), and Kam (Yeshé Gyaltsen).

13. Lama Dampa Sönam Gyaltsen (1312–1375) was four years younger than Longchenpa, yet the latter regarded him as a significant philosophical thinker, as revealed in a letter that Longchenpa wrote to Sönam Gyaltsen, in *Kloṅ-chen gSuṅ thor-bu*, vol. 1, pp. 360–363. (See Dudjom Rinpoche, *The Nyingma School of Tibetan Buddhism*, vol. 2, p. 49, n. 658)

14. Gönpo Maning Nakpo, or "the black lord who has no gender," is a major Dharma protector. "Maning" literally means "neuter." In this context it means "indivisible"; both masculine and feminine are embodied in this form of Mahakala (the Great Black One), the father of all the other Mahakalas. Most Mahakala lineages are masculine in emphasis. The absence of gender symbolizes that Maning is lord of both the protectors bound by karma (worldly protectors) and the wisdom (enlightened) protectors. Mahakala Maning possesses both skillful means and wisdom, compassion and emptiness, equally. Simply accomplishing Maning is like accomplishing one hundred, one thousand, or ten thousand deities because everything is complete in one form. Maning is usually depicted as blue-black in color, with three eyes, holding in the right hand a war banner and in the left a heart and noose, wearing a crown of skulls, and hair of black snakes.—Lopön Phurba Dorji, oral teaching.

15. Tsitta Marpo, or Tsiurmar, is the head of the Tsen class of beings, red in color, and very popular in the Tibetan province of Kham in eastern Tibet. The Tsen class is prevalent in North America and is associated with red rocks and mountains, which are numerous in North America. The others mentioned are probably local protectors.

CHAPTER FOUR: LEAVING SANGPHU AND DARK RETREAT

1. The reliquary of the great translator Ngok.

2. A thirty-line style of poetry composition with each line beginning with a word that starts with one of the letters of the Tibetan alphabet in order.

3. A great mahasiddha.

4. This is called "the dark retreat," an advanced Dzogchen practice wherein due to the prolonged immersion in total darkness, the light visions of tögal begin to manifest.

5. A reference to his perception of the lady as Tara.

6. *Sarva Durgati Purishodana Raja*, "The King of the Complete Removal of All Unfortunate Rebirths." Vairochana is called Sarvavid when he is at the center of a mandala related to the *Sarva Durgati Purishodana Tantra*.

7. This may have been the first empowerment that Longchenpa gave in his life.

CHAPTER FIVE: MEETING THE GURU KUMARADZA

1. A measure is about one quart.

CHAPTER SIX: VISIONS AND RETREATS

1. Found in his *The History of Lama Yangtig*. (See Longchen Rabjam, *The Practice of Dzogchen*, p. 151)

CHAPTER SEVEN: TURNING THE DHARMA WHEEL

1. "Butcheress Life Protectress"—a female Dharma protector.
2. The distinction being made here reflects the old style of Tibetan pronunciation, in which prefix and suffix letters were pronounced.
3. According to the Vinaya vows on the path of renunciation, monks do not partake of alcohol. However, in Tantra, the path of transformation, alcohol is one of the sacred samaya substances taken during a ganachakra. To honor both vows, it is first blessed as wisdom nectar to confer siddhis. Then usually monks will only dip a finger in the alcohol nectar, shake some off, and lick their finger, thus taking only a token amount. As in the story of Milarepa telling his new disciple, the monk Gampopa, to drink it all, this signified that Longchenpa would completely receive all the ordinary and supreme siddhis with none omitted.
4. Odé Küngyal is the deity of the mountain of the same name where the first king of Tibet, Nyatri Tsenpo of the Yarlung dynasty, is said to have descended from heaven around 127 BCE. Other accounts say that the place where the king came to earth was Yalashangbo.
5. The deity of a great mountain in Amdo province.
6. Also known as the Tseringma sisters.
7. Here the southwest refers to Longchenpa's future rebirth in the kingdom of Bhutan as Pema Lingpa.
8. Longchenpa's guru Kumaradza was an emanation of Vimalamitra, as was Longchenpa himself.
9. Another name for Pema Ledrel Tsal, Longchenpa's previous incarnation. His full name was Pangangpa Rinchen Tsultrim Dorjé.
10. Longchenpa's next life was as the tertön king Pema Lingpa, who was born in the central area of Chökor in Bumthang, Bhutan.
11. Akanishtha Buddhafield.
12. See pp. 40–41.
13. The wisdom empowerment is the third of the four empowerments in a higher tantra initiation. Among other blessings, it empowers the recipient to enhance and refine the bindu, or essence, also called the "red and white bodhichitta," and to practice the secret yoga of sexual union with a consort, or karma mudra, as the path of realizing the union of bliss and emptiness. In older times the third

empowerment was conferred using an actual consort; today it is usually bestowed using a painting of a consort, or by other symbolic representations. A visualized consort is called a "wisdom seal" or "jnana mudra."

14. In the tantric path of the Sarma, or New Translation, lineages, practice with an "action seal" (karma mudra), or consort, is considered to be indispensable for attaining the union of mother and son clear light, full buddhahood, in this lifetime. Hence, Naropa's famous quote: "No mahamudra without karma mudra." However, in Nyingma's Dzogchen system, it is not considered to be the ultimate path, but serves as skillful means to attract those with much desire, and to guide them by bringing that desire into the path as a preparation for the highest levels of the Dzogchen path. Longchenpa wrote about this in detail in *The Precious Treasury of the Supreme Vehicle*.

15. Princess Pemasal.

16. These were discovered later by Pema Lingpa.

17. This refers to the four volumes of the Vima Nyingthig.

CHAPTER EIGHT: TERMA REVELATIONS AND MIRACULOUS EVENTS

1. The innermost secret supplement for the Khandro Nyingthig.

2. A mind terma, *gongter* in Tibetan, is a category of terma discovered within the mindstream of the tertön. See Glossary.

3. Kangri Thökar; also phonetically rendered as Gangri Tökar.

4. Another name for Guru Rinpoché Padmasambhava.

5. This term may either refer to the youthful vase body or the heart from the perspective of the tögal view.

6. Another name for Dorjé Legpa (Skt. Vajra Sadhu), one of the main Dzogchen Dharma protectors.

7. *Sprul-bsgyur*; this compound belongs to the technical terminology of the yoga of the dream state, but is also applied to the manufacture of sacramental substances. (Dudjom Rinpoche, *The Nyingma School of Tibetan Buddhism*, vol. 2, p. 51, n. 681)

8. Remati carries a pouch of disease, an ancient form of germ warfare in India and later used by the Mongols as well, wherein tissue from humans and animals who died from plague or similar contagious illnesses are placed in a pouch and either thrown at enemies or tossed into the water supply of a populace. She uses such weapons on enemies of the Dharma. Although Remati is an enlightened Dharma protectress, not all of the spirits in her retinue are enlightened and may inflict disease on humans or animals.

CHAPTER NINE: WHITE SKULL SNOW MOUNTAIN

1. A reference to the visions of tögal.

2. Although he discovered the seed for this text at Chimphu, he actually transcribed

it at White Skull Snow Mountain; thus, it is said that he wrote it at White Skull Snow Mountain.

3. This means that one is cognizant of the emptiness and lack of inherent self-existence of offerer, offering, and recipient.

4. These are sacred days in the Tibetan Buddhist tantric calendar. The eighth day is sacred to Sangyé Menla (Skt. Bhaishajya; Guru Medicine Buddha); the tenth day is Guru Rinpoché Day; and the twenty-fifth day is Dakini Day.

5. Lotus King of Oddiyana. One of the eight manifestations of Guru Rinpoché, wherein he appears with crown as a young king.

6. Tib. *ösel tögal*, "crossing over to clear light."

7. The third vision of tögal.

8. The attainments mentioned in this paragraph are also signs indicating his attainment of the third vision.

9. The threefold purity of the emptiness of the one who dedicates, the act of dedication, and its recipient.

10. Around 1349 or 1350.

11. Also phonetically rendered as Künrig.

12. According to the Drikung Kagyu abbot Khenchen Konchog Gyaltshen, although Künrin was from Drikung, the seat of the Drikung Kagyu, he was not in any way a major figure within their lineage as one of political power or spiritual attainment.

13. The title Tai Situ, granted to him by the Mongols, means "Learned Instructor." This Tai Situ (1302–1364) became king of Tibet, and should not be confused with the Karma Kagyu tulku lineage of Tai Situs, one of the oldest tulku lineages in Tibet; the first of those, Tai Situ Chökyi Gyaltsen, lived 1377–1448, more than twenty-five years after these events.

14. Some references, notably H.V. Guenther in his introduction to *Kindly Bent to Ease Us*, vol. 1, p. xv, say that Künrin did in fact organize a revolt against Tai Situ.

CHAPTER TEN: SELF-EXILE IN BHUTAN

1. "Mani" means "jewel," a reference to the mantra of Avalokiteshvara (Skt.), or Chenrezig (Tib.), the bodhisattva of compassion, whose mantra is OM MANI PADME HUM.

2. Bumthang is one of the twenty dzongkhag (districts) comprising Bhutan. It is the most historic dzongkhag if the number of ancient temples and sacred sites is counted. Bumthang consists of the four mountain valleys of Ura, Chumé, Tang, and Chökhor (the latter is also known as Bumthang Valley), although occasionally the entire district is referred to as Bumthang Valley.

3. An ancient Buddhist kingdom on the Silk Road, in what is now within the Xinjiang province of China. To the Tibetans it was known as Li country.

4. Avalokiteshvara Jinasagara, or Red Chenrezig (Gyalwa Gyatso, Ocean of Conquerors), is one of the major yidams of the Karma Kagyu lineage.

5. Mahakala, one of the major Dharma protectors, a wrathful form of Avalokiteshvara.

6. Khenchen Chabdal Lhündrup was to become a most devoted disciple of Long-chenpa. He later was instrumental in arranging Longchenpa's return from exile in Bhutan, became a major lineage holder, and was the root guru of Longchenpa's son.

7. These log aqueducts are called *waa* in Bhutanese, and are still used today in Bhutan.

8. Tharpa Ling was apparently first established by Lorepa (1187–1250), a Drukpa Kagyu lama from Tibet. The temple that he founded is a small building below the main complex. In the fourteenth century another temple was founded by Longchen Rabjam.

9. In *The Life and Revelations of Pema Lingpa*, p. 37, Sarah Harding wrote the name as Kyipayak.

10. Heart Son.

11. The various accounts differ as to whether it was Gyalsé Drakpa Özer or his son (Longchenpa's grandson) Gyalsé Dawa Drakpa who was considered an emana-tion of Hayagriva. Adding to the confusion here is that both father and son were referred to as Dawa Drakpa.

12. Samling is the abbreviation of Samterling. It is believed that this nagtshang came to house a huge room of Longchenpa's termas, such as the cymbals of Rahula, statues, and scriptures. Some of the termas can be seen even today in Samling.

   When Dorji, the only son of Samling Ashi Choiten Zomba, was recruited as a noble (*garpa*) to serve in the court, it is believed that Samling Ashi gave Longchenpa's termas, one after another, as gifts to the court to relieve her son from courtly duties. Samling Nagtshang caught fire in 1982 (the fifteenth day of the eleventh Bhutanese month), but luckily the most important terma of the nagtshang, the seal of Longchenpa, was saved.

13. Now called Zhisar (New Settlement) after the Tibetan refugees who have settled in the area.

14. Protector's temple.

15. Called *naado.*

16. The author believes this to be a form of Hayagriva.

17. (*dong*–"face"; *kar*–"white"). So Domkhar is a corruption of Dongkar.

18. The throne of Longchenpa was later discovered in the basement of the monastery while it was being renovated. The throne, measuring 5.5 square feet and 1.7 feet in height, was found when the dirt of the basement was dug up to prevent the rotting of wooden planks.

19. *Glang dor.* The area of land in which one man with two yoked bulls could plow in a day.

20. *Chu zhing*, a special type of wetland that is more valuable as one can have two harvests per year.

21. This was how the Samling household, descended from Longchepa's son, Gyalsé

Tulku Drakpa Özer, came to possess some wetland and pastureland in Trongsa. The cattle of Samling continued to migrate to Wangleng during the winters up until the early 1980s, when the ownership of pastureland was returned to the local people after they complained that they could not grow any winter crop due to the presence of Samling cattle in the winter months, and that their "ignorant forefathers" had offered the pastureland to Longchenpa in return for his religious service. There were two pasturelands in Wangleng—a smaller one on a mountain slope surrounded by cliffs on three sides and a bigger one near the village. Chuzhing at Shengleng is still owned and farmed by the Samling household.—Dorji Penjore, *The Oral Construction of Exile Life and Times of Künkhyen Longchen Rabjam in Bumthang.*

22. Phajo Drukgom Zhikpo (1184–1251), a great master of the Drukpa Kagyu School. (See Jampa Mackenzie Stewart, *The Life of Gampopa,* p. 131)

CHAPTER ELEVEN: RETURN TO TIBET

1. Also called Buddhashri.
2. Lhodrak is an exceptionally sacred place in southern Tibet near the border of Bhutan. Perhaps best known as the home of Marpa the Translator, and the place where Milarepa built his tower, it was also one of the sacred spots of Guru Rinpoché; Namkhai Nyingpo, one of his twenty-five close disciples spent much time there. Longchenpa's root guru, Kumaradza, spent much time at Lhodrak Kharchu in a small monastery built by Kumaradza's root guru, Melong Dorjé. The great Drukpa Kagyu lama Pema Karpo also stayed there and restored the monastery.
3. The Tripitaka, or Three Baskets: Vinaya, Sutra, and Abhidharma.

CHAPTER TWELVE: FINAL DAYS AND PARINIRVANA

1. The Yangthig Yizhin Norbu, also known as the Lama Yangthig. This text is a commentary on both the Vima Nyingthig and Khandro Nyingthig.
2. "Usually it is considered to be harmful to the rainbow body transference for it to occur in a great gathering; it is apparently meant to occur in a more private way."—Yangthang Tulku, *The Nyingthig Yabshi Empowerments.*
3. Some say that the year he died was actually 1364.
4. This refers to the fourth vision of tögal, where all phenomena are exhausted into dharmata.
5. Most sources list the year of Longchenpa's passing as 1363. Dudjom Rinpoché gives the date at December 25, 1363. However, calculating according to the Tibetan calendar cited in the text, the accurate date would be as given above.
6. Parts of this part of the text were excerpted from Khenpo Namdrol Rinpoche,

The Three Statements That Strike the Vital Point: The Last Testament of Prahevajra (Garab Dorje), p. 215.

7. Relics, pearl-like in color and shape, that only appear in the cremation ashes of highly realized beings.
8. Larger relics.
9. In Dudjom Rinpoche, *The Nyingma School of Tibetan Buddhism*, vol. 2, p. 51, n. 695: "Upper demons (*steng-gdon*) afflict the brain, causing epilepsy, stroke and nervous disorders."

CHAPTER THIRTEEN: HIS LEGACY

1. In Sarah Harding, *The Life and Revelations of Pema Lingpa*, p. 39, the Eighth Sungtrul Rinpoché (a speech emanation of Pema Lingpa) tells an odd story of an incarnation before Pema Lingpa near Tharpa Ling in Bhutan as a boy named Tokar who was killed at the age of seven when struck in the head by a rock while trying to steal peas from a neighbor's field. He then went to the Glorious Mountain of Chamara where he dwelled for twenty-five human years with Guru Rinpoché. He was then commanded to return to benefit beings.
2. Mantra Protectress Ekajati.
3. Tib. *Dzogchen Longsal Gyi Kor.*
4. See ch. 1, n. 21.
5. There are different definitions of the three kinds of faith in Buddhism. One is: (1) a conviction that something is; (2) a determination to accomplish one's goals; and (3) a sense of joy deriving from the other two. Another is: (1) sincere interest in the Three Jewels as the guide on the path; (2) longing and eagerness to pursue the path; and (3) trust in karma and the Four Noble Truths.
6. A reference to tögal practice.
7. Nyoshul Khenpo, *A Marvelous Garland of Rare Gems*, p. 635, n. 7: "Normally, a master passes away before the next incarnation appears, but in some instances it has been accepted that the master's death did not precede the birth of the reincarnation."
8. The prophecy is found in his father's biography earlier in this chapter.
9. In *Masters of Meditation and Miracles* Tulku Thondup states it slightly differently, with Do Khyentsé Rinpoché as his body incarnation, Patrul Rinpoché as his speech incarnation, and Jamyang Khyentsé Wangpo as his mind incarnation.
10. Also known as Khenpo Ngagi Wangpo. Khenchen Ngawang Palzangpo, or simply Khenpo Ngaga. For a complete biography of this amazing guru, see Nyoshul Khenpo, *A Marvelous Garland of Rare Gems*, pp. 247–256.
11. Also known as Dzongsar Khyentsé Chökyi Lodrö.
12. For a complete list of his works, see Nyoshul Khenpo, *A Marvelous Garland of Rare Gems*, pp. 132–144.

13. I.e., dharmadhatu.

14. Published by Padma Publishing as *The Precious Treasury of the Way of Abiding.*

15. See also *Trilogy of Natural Ease,* Wikipedia: http://en.wikipedia.org/wiki/Trilogy_of_Natural_Ease

16. Dorjé Ziji Tsal (Vajra of Dynamic Brilliance) was the full name given.

17. Another name for Padmasambhava, Guru Rinpoché.

18. From the *History of the Lama Yangtig,* excerpted in Longchen Rabjam, *The Practice of Dzogchen,* p. 166.

In Praise of Longchen Rabjam

1. These are the great Indian commentators on the Buddha's teachings. The Six Ornaments are Nagarjuna, Aryadeva, Asanga, Vasubandhu, Dignaga, and Dharmakirti. The Two Supreme Ones are Gunaprabha and Shakyaprabha.

2. Literally, "frolicked in his throat."

3. Tibetan word for "translators."

4. I.e., Dzogchen.

5. Khenpo Shenga himself was blessed with such a vision.

Glossary

Akanishtha (Skt.; Tib. *Ogmin*) "Nothing Higher." This name is used to apply to two different realms: one transcendent and the other samsaric. In the former context Akanishtha is the name of the highest of the buddhafields, often used as a synonym for the dharmakaya. In the latter context it is also the name of the highest realm of the form-realm gods.

Amitabha (Skt.) The Buddha of Boundless Light. Amitabha is the dharmakaya buddha of Sukhavati (Skt.), or Dewachen (Tib.), the Western Pure Land of Great Bliss. Due to Amitabha's compassionate motivation while on the path to buddhahood to not attain enlightenment until he gained the capacity whereby all sentient beings who had faith in him can be reborn in his buddhafield, he is one of the most popularly venerated of all the buddhas.

Among the five buddha families, Amitabha is the head of the Lotus family, whose realm is to the west. His sambhogakaya form is Avalokiteshvara and his nirmanakaya form is Guru Rinpoché Padmasambhava.

Amitayus (Skt.) The Buddha of Boundless Life. Amitayus is a sambhogakaya form of Amitabha and his meditation is practiced to increase one's lifespan.

Anuyoga (Skt.) Anuyoga is the second of the three inner tantras in the Nyingma School. Anuyoga places its emphasis on the completion stage (Tib. *dzogrim*), and so its practices focus on working with the channels, winds, and drops to realize the vajra body, speech, and mind of buddhahood.

Atiyoga (Skt.; Tib. *dzogpa chenpo*) Atiyoga, or Maha Ati, is the third and highest of the three inner tantras, and the ninth of the nine yanas. Atiyoga is one of the Sanskrit names for Dzogchen, or Great Perfection, the other being Mahasandhi. *See* Dzogchen.

Avalokiteshvara (Skt.; Tib. *Chenrezig*) The bodhisattva of compassion and a sambhogakaya form of Amitabha Buddha. In the Mahayana scriptures Avalokiteshvara was a human disciple of Shakyamuni Buddha. It was he who, upon his enlightenment, gave the Prajnaparamita *Heart Sutra*. His compassionate vows became the foundation of the bodhisattva path in our time.

bardo (Tib.) The intermediate, or in-between, state. Although *bardo* commonly refers to the state between death and rebirth, there are actually six bardos: (1) the bardo of dying; (2) the bardo of dharmata (the luminosity immediately following death); (3) the bardo of becoming (where one is drawn toward rebirth); (4) the bardo between birth and death (life in one of the six realms); (5) the bardo of dreaming (the state between falling asleep and waking); (6) the bardo of meditation (samadhi).

bindu (Skt.; Tib.: *thiglé*) Drop, dot, semen, essence, sphere, circle. The bindus, or drops, within the body are about the size of sesame seeds and are more substantive than prana. Although substantial, they are clear like a crystal or diamond, and magnificently bright. There are two basic types of drops: the white drops and the red drops. The white drops are the pure essence of the male seminal fluid (sperm). The red drops are related to the pure essence of the female menstrual blood (ovum). There are gross and subtle aspects to the drops. The gross, or substantive, form of the red and white drops flows through the nadis, or channels. The subtle drops exist within the center of the heart chakra, which is penetrated by the central channel (Tib. *uma*).

The seat of the white drop is in the crown chakra at the top of the head, and it is from here that the semen originates. The seat of the red drop is in the navel chakra, and it is from here that the blood originates. The red drop is also the source of bodily warmth, and is the foundation for developing the inner heat of *tummo*. The energy of the drops has both a temporary and ultimate value. Its temporary value is to produce the state of great bliss for anuyoga practitioners. Within that experience of the blissful state, one uses the mind of great bliss to meditate on emptiness. This is the ultimate value, the realization of the yidam, whose essential nature is bliss inseparable from emptiness.

In some contexts, *bindu* specifically refers to the sexual essences, i.e., the semen and menstrual blood. It may also be referred to as the red and white bodhichitta. Conservation of these substances is considered vital to the path of anuyoga.

Within the Nyingthig levels of Dzogchen there is a distinction between the genuine wisdom bindus, which reside in the heart and the pure light channels, and the causal relative impure bindus related to the red and white drops. There are many distinctions made regarding the variety of types of wisdom bindus in terms of the ground, path, and result. Essentially, the genuine wisdom bindus are what one is concerned with in Dzogchen, and in particular for the practitioner of tögal. The essence of this bindu is clear light, abiding as kayas, light, and rays (the light's radiance).

Although indwelling, through observing the key points of tögal practice the bindus from within are rendered evident in the space in front of one with five-colored light auras surrounding them. The bindus evolve in a natural process through the stages of the four visions of tögal. Longchenpa discusses the nature and purpose of the bindus within the context of Dzogchen quite extensively in *The Precious Treasury of the Supreme Vehicle* and *The Precious Treasury of Words and Meanings*.

bodhichitta (Skt.; Tib. *jangchub kyi sem*) *Bodhi* means "awakening," while *chitta* means "mind." Thus, *bodhichitta* means "awakening mind." In the sutras and tantras there are two types of bodhichitta: absolute, or ultimate, bodhichitta and relative bodhichitta. According to Gampopa, absolute bodhichitta is the nondual realization of emptiness inseparable from compassion, which is radiant, unshakeable, and beyond concepts. Relative bodhichitta is the compassionate mind of the bodhisattva, the aspiration to become enlightened for the sake of all living beings. Included within this is the practice of the six paramitas and the practice of the Four Immeasurables (*brahmaviharas*): love, compassion, joy in the joy of others, and equanimity. Relative bodhichitta has two aspects: aspiration bodhichitta and perseverance bodhichitta. Aspiration bodhichitta means forming the wish and intention to become enlightened to benefit all beings; perseverance bodhichitta is performing the actions of body, speech, and mind to actually realize that goal.

In Dzogchen there is a specific definition of arousing bodhichitta. According to Nyoshul Khen Rinpoché, "What is arousing bodhichitta according to the uncommon approach of Dzogchen? . . . the key point here is that all these sentient beings are recognized as having within themselves inherent wisdom, self-abiding dharmakaya—the self-knowing rigpa, the unity of space and wisdom, that is the actual lama who is the all-pervasive sovereign, the glorious primordial buddha Samantabhadra. That actually resides within us all, and so we wish: 'May I be able to bring all sentient beings to the level where they realize this.'" (See *A Marvelous Garland of Rare Gems,* p. xxiv)

bodhisattva (Skt.; Tib. *jangchub sempa*) Awakening hero. One who is following the Mahayana path of the six paramitas and is cultivating bodhichitta, both relative and absolute. One formally takes the bodhisattva vows from one's spiritual master, and thereafter renews the vows daily with the aspiration to attain enlightenment not merely for oneself, but for the sake of all sentient beings, and to continue to be reborn within samsara until all beings have attained liberation.

body of great transference (Tib. *phowa chenpo*) Also called "the rainbow body of great transference (*ja lu phowa chenpo*)." This is the highest of the accomplishments of tögal, where the yogi(ni) dissolves his/her body into light—the essence of all the elements—and then lives on for centuries with the ability to appear in different forms to benefit sentient beings. This body of great transference was accomplished by such beings as Padmasambhava, Vimalamitra, and Chetsun Sengé Wangchuk. *See* rainbow body.

buddhafield The realm or abode of a buddha.

buddhahood Full and complete enlightenment.

charyatantra The second of the three outer tantras. It is also the fifth yana in the nine-yana classification common to the Nyingma School. It is called the vehicle of charya, or "conduct," tantra because it gives equal emphasis to the outer actions of body and speech and the inner cultivation of samadhi (mind). Another name for it is the "tantra of both" (Skt. *ubhaya tantra*) because its view accords with yogatantra, while its conduct is similar to that of kriyatantra.

Chemchok Heruka (Tib.; Skt. *Mahottara*) Chemchok Heruka is the central deity in the mandala of the fifty-eight wrathful deities, and is the wrathful aspect of Samantabhadra. Chemchok Heruka is also the main deity in the mandala of the Kagyé.

Chöd (Tib.) Literally, "to cut." In the yogic context it means to cut the basis of attachment to the illusion of a separate and inherently existing self through the ritual offering of one's body to all beings—and to cut the four maras in particular.

The Chöd practice is based upon the revelations of the Prajnaparamita Sutras. It was introduced into Tibet by the Indian guru Padampa Sangyé, and was developed by his chief Tibetan disciple, the great Tibetan yogini Machig Labdrön. Machig Labdrön became so renowned that students and teachers traveled from India to Tibet to receive her Chöd teachings.

Because of the shamanistic character of the Chöd practice, some have speculated that it was adopted from Bön, the native religion of Tibet. However, according to Lopön Tenzin Namdak, one of the major living Bön teachers, the Bön also learned Chöd from Padampa Sangyé, and made it a part of their tradition at the same time as the Buddhists.

clear light (Tib. *ösel*) Also translated as "luminosity," "radiance," or "utter lucidity."

The true, unborn, unfabricated, and uncontrived nature of mind, cognizant and present throughout all of samsara and nirvana. There are two aspects to clear light: empty clear light, which is like a clear, open sky; and manifest clear light, which appears as the five lights, images, and the like.

In the Great Perfection this term is sometimes used with capital letters—Clear Light Great Perfection—as a proper name for the Dzogchen teachings. In the Great Perfection it has different meanings in different situations. According to the oral teachings of Lama Dechen Yeshe Wangmo, all appearances are the continuity or radiance of primordial purity—*kadag*. Teachings on primordial purity are on emptiness, as in other schools, such as Mahamudra and Madhyamaka. The teachings on spontaneous presence— *lhündrup*—are different from that of other schools; phenomena are coequal with the essence as primordial purity's luminosity, as appearances manifesting from the ground of being.

In Dzogchen there is also a further distinction made between the inner radiance of the ground and the inner radiance of the path. These are called "the mother clear light" and "the path clear light," respectively.

Just as the term "lucidity" can refer to external light, it can also be used to describe the most profound level of mental clarity, the illuminating quality of awake awareness, of pure knowing that clears away the darkness of mental dullness, confusion, and ignorance. This has been eloquently described by Trulzhik Adeu Rinpoche and Tulku Urgyen Rinpoche:

"In addition, in the Prajnaparamita, the Buddha says, 'Mind does not exist as mind, but as a nature that is luminous wakefulness.' This luminosity refers to the naked quality that is able to know. Even though it is not a thing, there is still an unimpeded ability to know. That is called 'luminosity'—empty, yet able to know." (*Skillful Grace*, p. 119)

clear light vajra essence A name for the Nyingthig teachings of the Great Perfection.

crossing over (Tib. *tögal*) *See* tögal.

cutting through (Tib. *trekchö*) *See* trekchö.

daka (Skt.; Tib. *khandro*) Literally, "sky goer," meaning one who dances in the sky of the vast space of wisdom. The Tibetan term often denotes a male semiwrathful yidam. One of the Three Roots of tantric refuge, dakas are beings who are related to enlightened activity and skillful means. Depending on the context, it can refer to the ideal of a male Vajrayana practitioner as spiritual warrior or as the hero who conquers the four maras; to living people (where it is sometimes used as an honorific or part of a name); to legendary or mythical figures from the past; or to purely spiritual beings. Dakas may also be messengers or Dharma protectors, depending on the context. Dakas are typically described in consort with dakinis, their feminine counterparts.

dakini (Skt.; Tib. *khandroma*) Literally, "sky goer," meaning one who dances in the sky of the vast space of wisdom. The term *dakini* usually refers to a class of beings that embody female enlightened energy. They represent the wisdom of emptiness, the basic fertile womb of space, the innate wisdom out of which both samsara and nirvana arise. They can be benevolent, or also playful and tricky, or even dangerous, yet their essence is compassionate, like a loving mother; they can also hold powerful magnetizing erotic energy, expressing the enlightened aspects of passionate wakefulness and bliss. There are both enlightened dakinis and worldly dakinis. Female lamas and the spiritual consorts of male lamas are also called *dakinis*.

Desire Realm One of three realms of existence within samsara, comprising the lower god realm, demigods (or asuras), humans, animals, hungry ghosts (or pretas), and hell beings. It is called the Desire Realm because beings are reborn and experience suffering within this realm due to gross attachment and desire. *See also* six realms, Form Realm, and Formless Realm.

Dharma (Skt.; Tib. *chö*) Truth, law, way, path. The teachings of the buddhas. In other contexts, *dharma* refers to things, to phenomena, to mental and physical objects.

Dharma protectors (Skt. *dharmapalas;* Tib. *chökyong*) Also translated as "guardians." One of the best descriptions I have read anywhere on the Dharma protectors is cited below. It comes from an Internet blog by Hun Lye:

> It is said that there are three kinds of protectors. They are dharmapalas, lokapalas and ksetrapalas. Respectively they translate to "dharma-protectors," "worldly-protectors," and "field-protectors." Dharma-protectors are those who are highly advanced on the Path. From Vajrayana's point of view, these beings are actually manifestations of the [enlightened] activities of the Buddhas. Some of these beings are considered Buddhas while some are on different levels of the Bodhisattva path. For example, Mahakala and Ekazati [Ekajati] are both considered fully enlightened beings, while someone like Dorje Legpa is considered a tenth stage bodhisattva. The worldly-protectors refer to beings who have pledged to protect the teachings and practitioners. These include powerful worldly gods, local spirits, energies, and other beings. It is said that sometimes these beings do not even fully accept the teachings of the Buddha. They are in other words as deluded as we are— some of them more, others less. Field-protectors are usually associated with very specific places or buildings. In Tibet, families live in the same place and house for hundreds of years. As time passes, it is believed that there are certain protectors especially connected with that particular house, clan, or family. Spiritually, both the worldly- and field-protectors are much lower than the dharma-protectors. Both the worldly- and field-protectors are not particularly related to Dharma in the same way as dharma-protectors are.

Hun Lye also further describes the Dharma protectors as different forms of energy that are latent within us. (For the full description, see www.sacred-texts.com/bud/tib/protect.htm)

dharmadhatu (Skt.; Tib. *chöying*) The basic space of phenomena. The unborn realm of all-encompassing space in which all things appear to arise, exist, and cease.

dharmakaya (Skt.; Tib. *chöku*) *See* four bodies of a buddha.

Dharmakirti Dharmakirti International in Tuscon, Arizona, offers a pertinent bio of this important figure on their website: "Dharmakirti (seventh century CE) was one of the Six Ornaments, or six great commentators on the teachings of the Buddha, and one of the most important Buddhist philosophers of all times. He was born to a South Indian Brahmin family. Later he studied at Nalanda University, where he eventually became a teacher and was one of the Buddhist founders of Indian philosophical logic (*pramana*). His writings on *pramana* treat basic questions concerning the nature of knowledge, its forms, and its relation to the external world.

"He profoundly influenced Mahayana Buddhism and South Asian philosophy as a whole. Dharmakirti was one of the principal spokesmen of the Yogachara, Chittamatra, or Mind Only School of Indian Buddhist philosophy, which greatly influenced Tibetan Buddhism, especially the Nyingma School and Dzogchen. His Seven Treatises on Valid Cognition, often cited in teachings by His Holiness the Dalai Lama, are a basic part of the monastic curriculum even today." (See Dharmakirti.org/about_dharmakirti.htm)

dharmapala (Skt.; Tib. *chökyong*) *See* Dharma protectors.

dharmata (Skt.; Tib. *chönyid*) Suchness. The pure nature of reality, phenomena, and mind as they are, without elaboration.

Dignaga Dignaga (circa 480–540 CE) was one of the Six Ornaments, or six great commentators on the Dharma. Dignaga was one of the four great disciples of Vasubandhu, who each surpassed their teacher in a particular field. Dignaga was more learned than Vasubandhu in the field of valid cognition (*pramana*). One of his disciples, Ishvarasena, later became the teacher of Dharmakirti.

Dorjé Legpa (Tib.; Skt. *Vajra Sadhu*) One of the three principal Dharma protectors of the Dzogchen lineage, along with Ekajati and Rahula. Dorjé Legpa is a highly developed being of the Nyen Class among the Eight Classes of Dharma Protectors. Originally a protector of the Bön Dzogchen tradition, he is still supplicated by the Bön as "A-se." Initially he was opposed to the spread of Buddhism in Tibet by Padmasambhava, but later was subjugated and made an oath to Guru Rinpoché to protect Buddhist Dzogchen practitioners.

Among the various protectors, Dorjé Legpa is unique in that he may be called upon for worldly protection and help as well as spiritual protection. In particular, he is also the patron protector of sportsmen and gamblers. He is often depicted as black in color, riding on a lion, holding a nine-pointed vajra in his right hand and the heart of the enemies of the Dharma in his left hand. This is the way he manifested at the time when he swore his oath of allegiance to Guru Rinpoché.

Dorjé Yudrönma (Tib.) Dorjé Yudrönma is a wisdom deity who manifests out of her compassion in the form of a protectress.

drops (Tib. *thiglé*) *See* bindu.

drubchen (Tib.) Literally, "great accomplishment." An intensive group deity-yoga practice retreat, usually lasting one to two weeks, and including both monks and nuns, as well as male and female lay practitioners. During the drubchen retreat the prayers and mantra of the yidam are recited continuously, twenty-four hours a day, by retreatants. According to Gangteng Tulku Rinpoché, "The merit and blessings generated, even within such a short period of time, are so immense that it is said to be the same as undertaking a traditional three-year retreat."

Dzambhala (Tib.) *See* Vaishravana.

Dzogchen or **Dzogpa Chenpo** (Tib.; Skt. *Atiyoga, Maha Ati, Mahasandhi*) The Tibetan word *Dzogchen* is an abbreviation of *Dzogpa Chenpo. Dzogpa* means "perfection" or "completion." *Chenpo* means "great." Therefore, it is usually translated as "the Great Perfection."

First and foremost, the Great Perfection is the ground of being, our true nature of mind and the basic space of phenomena: unborn, undying, perfect as it is, primordially pure, stainless, spontaneously present yet empty, our buddha nature, the union of awareness and emptiness. Its perfection is that it encompasses all the inseparable qualities of the three kayas of the buddhas: its essence is empty, corresponding to the dharmakaya; its nature is spontaneously present luminous clarity, corresponding to the sambhogakaya; and its compassion emanates unimpededly as resonating responsiveness, corresponding to the nirmanakaya.

Secondly, Dzogchen is the name of the path to recognizing our primordial indwelling wisdom (*yeshé*) and intrinsic awareness (*rigpa*). As the supreme path, Dzogchen is the ninth of the nine yanas of the Nyingma School. It has been absorbed into the other Tibetan lineages as well; practitioners such as the Fifth Dalai Lama of the Gelugpa School and the Third Karmapa, Rangjung Dorjé, of the Kagyu School were famous Dzogchen practitioners, and outstanding practitioners are found among the Sakyapas as well. It is also a central and highly developed practice in Bön, the native religion of Tibet, and is said to be practiced in other dimensions, too.

In Sanskrit, Dzogchen is called *Atiyoga* or *Mahasandhi. Ati* means the pinnacle, like ascending a mountain and reaching the peak, from which there is no higher outlook; one has finished one's journey and is complete, with an unobstructed and clear view of all that is below. The term *Mahasandhi* means the gathering of all the essences, the quintessence, signifying that Dzogchen is the heart essence (*nyingthig*) of all the teachings.

There are three classes, or cycles, of Dzogchen teachings: Semdé (Mind Class), Longdé (Space Class), and Mengagdé (Oral Instruction Class).

The Mengagdé Class of teachings is further subdivided into Outer, Inner, Secret, and Innermost Secret. It is in the Innermost Secret level that Dzogchen's extraordinary approach to practice has its two branches: the way of trekchö and the way of tögal. In trekchö, the approach is based upon cutting through to the primordial purity of mind (*kadag*), through which the lazy can reach liberation without effort (although it is not easy), while the approach of tögal is based upon surpassing the pinnacle to directly realize spontaneous presence (*lhündrup*), through which the diligent can reach liberation through effort. Founded upon a strong foundation of trekchö, one's tögal practice matures through the stages of the four visions, culminating in full and complete buddhahood.

At the time of fruition, the special sign of accomplishing trekchö is that one's body dissolves into atoms and one's mind is absorbed into dharmata. In tögal, the highest accomplishment is that one attains full and complete buddhahood in the special form of the immortal rainbow body of great transference in order to benefit beings.

As the highest of the nine yanas, Dzogchen has several extraordinary and unique attributes. Firstly, it is the only yana whose path is based not upon ordinary mind (*sem*), but rather upon rigpa, intrinsic awareness. Second, due to the first point, the student is taught to discern the difference between ordinary mind and rigpa. Third, the student is directly introduced to rigpa through the pointing-out instructions of the master through various skillful methods. Fourth, although there is direct introduction of rigpa, this does not mean there is no preparation for this. However, there is no hard and fast rule of preliminaries that is applied to all students, nor is it required that students must proceed and be initiated from step to step and level to level before receiving the higher teaching. In Dzogchen, according to Namkhai Norbu Rinpoché, ". . . the disciple is given the opportunity to enter at the highest level right away, and only if the capacity for this level is lacking is it necessary to work down to find a level of practice that will enable whatever difficulties there may be to be overcome so that the disciple can proceed to contemplation itself. . . . [Garab Dorjé] said that the first thing to be done was for the master to give a Direct Introduction; and that the disciple should try to enter into the primordial state, discovering how it is for him- or herself, so as to no longer be in any doubt about it; and then the disciple should try to continue in that state. As and when obstacles arise, the practitioner applies a practice to overcome them. If one finds one lacks a certain capacity, one sets about doing the practice that will help to develop it. Thus, one can see that the principle of Dzogchen relies on the awareness of the practitioner in deciding what must be done, rather than on a rule compulsorily applied to one and all. This is how it must be in Dzogchen . . ." (*The Crystal and the Way of Light*, p. 83).

Fifth, while the view of the trekchö path is said to be the same as that of Mahamudra and Madhyamaka with its focus on primordial purity (*kadag*), the path of tögal is unique to Dzogchen in its emphasis on direct perception of spontaneous presence, the pure appearances of the ground of being. The result of tögal practice—the rainbow body—is also unique.

Sixth, in the other yanas, the three kayas—dharmakaya, sambhogakaya, and nirmanakaya —are the result of the practice, while in Dzogchen the three kayas are part of the path, but not the result. In Dzogchen the resultant state of awakening occurs in the basic space of primordial purity. One who is experiencing the resultant state of the three kayas is still on the path. Even that, all the phenomena of samsara and nirvana, must resolve into the state of primordial purity.

These are but some of the unique features of the Dzogchen way.

earth terma treasure (Tib. *sater*) Earth terma treasures are hidden sacred texts or objects that were physically concealed by Guru Padmasambhava and Yeshé Tsogyal or by other masters for discovery at a later date. They may be concealed in rocks, trees, caves, lakes, pillars, and so forth. Their discovery and extraction often take place under miraculous circumstances, and are sometimes revealed publicly. *See also* mind terma treasure, terma, tertön.

Eight Commands (Tib. *Kagyé*) A practice taught by Guru Rinpoché Padmasambhava wherein all the main yidams are gathered into one mandala. *See* Eight Sadhana Teachings, Eight Vidyadharas, Gathering of Sugatas.

Eight Sadhana Teachings The Eight Sadhana Teachings refers to the eight chief yidam deities of Mahayoga and their corresponding tantras and sadhanas that were transmitted to Guru Rinpoché by the eight Indian vidyadharas. These tantras are: *Manjushri Body, Lotus Speech, Vishuddha Mind, Nectar Quality, Kilaya Activity, Liberating Sorcery of Mother Deities, Maledictory Fierce Mantra,* and *Mundane Worship.* Often the name refers to a single practice involving complex mandalas with numerous deities. *See also* Gathering of Sugatas, Sadhana Section.

Eight Vidyadharas Manjushrimitra, Nagarjuna, Hungkara, Vimalamitra, Prabhahasti, Dhana Sanskrita, Shintam Garbha, and Guhyachandra. These are the eight yogis who each received one of the yidam sadhanas of the Kagyé cycle. *See* Eight Commands.

Ekajati (Skt.; Tib. *Ralchigma*) "One knot of hair." One of the principal protectresses of the Dzogchen lineage who displays herself as a member of the mamo class, one of the eight classes of demons. She is depicted as dark red in color with one eye, one tooth, one breast, and one knot of hair. Her name is also transcribed as *Ekadzati*.

empowerment (Skt. *abhisheka*; Tib. *wong*) The three prerequisites for tantric practice are: empowerment, or initiation into the particular tantra; the oral transmission blessing (*lung*) in the form of a ritual reading of the text to be studied or the tantric sadhana to be practiced; and the oral pith instructions (*tri*) as a commentary on the meaning of the text or on how to correctly perform the practice.

During an empowerment the vajra master goes into the various samadhis required in the practice, wherein he verbally, energetically, and symbolically transmits the experience—the fruit of the practice—to the initiate. The initiate is usually unable to sustain the peak of this experience, but the transmission is a blessing that plants a seed, or experiential frame of reference, to be deepened through continued practice, until the experience is finally stabilized and ripens into full perfect realization.

Form Realm A higher god realm, where beings are free from the desire of the Desire Realm, but still have attachment to subtler forms and sensations. There is neither smell nor taste in the Form Realm. The beings born here have cultivated various meditative absorptions; they are huge and live extremely long lives.

Formless Realm The highest god realms, where beings have cut off attachment to both the Desire and Form Realm objects but are still fixated on the bliss of meditation. They have no bodies since they have transcended form.

four bodies of a buddha The four bodies, or four kayas, of a buddha are: (1) the dharmakaya, or ultimate truth body, corresponding to the mind aspect of a buddha; (2) the sambhogakaya, or complete enjoyment body, corresponding to the speech and light aspects of a buddha; (3) the nirmanakaya, or emanation body, corresponding to the physically appearing body of a buddha; and, (4) the svabhavikakaya, the essential or nature body, representing the inseparability of the first three bodies.

Sometimes only the first three kayas are mentioned: the dharmakaya, sambhogakaya, and nirmanakaya (trikaya). Other times only two kayas are mentioned: the dharmakaya and the rupakaya, or form body. In this instance, the rupakaya encompasses both the sambhogakaya and the nirmanakaya. These are sometimes spoken of in the context of the "two benefits": one realizes the ultimate nondual truth body of dharmakaya for one's own benefit; and one realizes the relative manifestations of the rupakaya in order to benefit others.

four lamps Also translated as the "four luminosities." The four lamps are a part of tögal practice. They all serve as a metaphor for awareness or knowing which, like a lamp, illuminates itself and all phenomena with which it comes into contact. The four lamps are: (1) the lamp of perfectly pure basic space; (2) the lamp of the empty bindus; (3) the lamp of self-emergent prajna; and, (4) the lamp of the far-reaching watery lasso. *See also* six lamps.

four maras Four of the major obstacles to spiritual practice and enlightenment. These are: (1) skandha-mara, falsely perceiving the five skandhas as an inherently existing self; (2) klesha-mara, being overcome by the mental confusion of conflicting emotions; (3) mrtyu-mara, death, which causes a break in spiritual practice unless the practitioner is able to use the experience of dying and death to achieve enlightenment; (4) devaputra-mara, the "mara of the gods' son," where life becomes so pleasurable that one is distracted from spiritual practice.

four visions The four visions are the four major stages of tögal practice: (1) direct experience of dharmata; (2) increase of visionary experience; (3) awareness (rigpa) reaching full measure; and (4) exhaustion of appearances into dharmata.

ganachakra (Skt.; Tib. *tsog* or *tsogkyi khorlo*) A gathering of tantric practitioners for a sacred ritual feast offering.

Gathering of Sugatas (Tib. *Kagyé Deshek Dupa*) An important cycle of teachings connected to the Sadhana Section of Mahayoga. The tantras belonging to this cycle are found in vol. OM of the Nyingma *Gyübum* as well as in the revelations of Nyang Ral Nyima Özer. These teachings were transmitted by Samantabhadra, manifest in the form of the peaceful Vajrasattva and wrathful Chemchok Heruka.

The Lord of Secrets compiled and entrusted them to the dakini Leykyi Wangmo. She concealed these tantras in the stupa Enchanting Mound, and later transmitted them to the Eight Vidyadharas, one teaching to each master: *Manjushri Body* to Manjushrimitra, *Lotus Speech* to Nagarjuna, *Vishuddha Mind* to Hungkara, *Nectar Quality* to Vimalamitra, *Kilaya Activity* to Prabhahasti, *Liberating Sorcery of Mother Deities* to Dhana Sanskrita, *Maledictory Fierce Mantra* to Shintam Garbha, and *Mundane Worship* to Guhyachandra. Each of these vidyadharas later transmitted their teachings to Padmasambhava, who then became the main holder of all.

Great Perfection *See* Dzogchen.

guru *See* lama.

Guru Drakpo "Wrathful Guru." One of the Eight Manifestations of Guru Rinpoché Padmasambhava.

Hayagriva (Skt.; Tib. *Tamdrin*) Hayagriva is a wrathful manifestation of Avalokiteshvara, the bodhisattva of compassion. Associated with the Lotus family, he is depicted as red in color with a neighing horse's head emerging from his own. He is one of the eight deities of Kagyé.

Heart Essence (Tib. *nyingthig*) *See* nyingthig.

inner radiance (Tib. *ösel*) *See* clear light, youthful vase body.

Jambudvipa (Tib. *Dzambuling*) In Hindu and Buddhist cosmology, it is one of the four continents of the phenomenal world, located to the south of Mount Meru, the mountain that lies at the center of the world. Jambudvipa is the world where humans live.

kadag *See* primordial purity.

Kagyé *See* Eight Commands, Gathering of Sugatas.

kaya (Skt.; Tib. *ku*) Literally, "body." *See* four bodies of a buddha.

khandro *See* dakini.

Khechara A dakini realm.

kriyatantra The first of the three lower tantras. Kriyatantra places a great emphasis on ritual and purity. One visualizes the deity as separate and outside oneself; in the kriyatantra view one is considered to be inferior to the deity, who imparts wisdom to us.

kusali (Skt.; also rendered as *kusula* or *kusuli*) Mendicant practitioner. The kusali stands in contrast to the pandita; the pandita follows the path of scholarly inquiry and intellectual understanding of the teachings, whereas the kusali seeks direct understanding through the pith instructions on how to practice in order to obtain the experiential results of realization.

lama (Skt. *guru*) The term *lama* can apply to both monastic and lay teachers. Literally, "teacher-mother," it implies that the teacher who gives spiritual teachings that can guide one to buddhahood is showing kindness as great as or greater than that of one's own mother. The title is usually reserved for those who have completed the traditional three-year meditation retreat.

leaping over *See* tögal.

lhündrup *See* spontaneous presence.

Longdé (Tib.) The Space Class of Dzogchen teachings. Garab Dorjé transmitted all of the Dzogchen teachings to Manjushrimitra, who then subdivided them into three series or classes: Semdé, Longdé, and Mengagdé.
  According to Chögyal Namkhai Norbu, "The three classes are three ways of presenting the teaching, each with its corresponding methods of practice; the aim of all three, however, is to lead to final realization. Longdé means the 'series of space.' In this

instance 'space' refers to the primordial dimension of emptiness which serves as a base for manifesting the clarity of the practitioner." (Excerpted from http://tsegyalgar. org/theteachings/dzogchen/). *See also* Semdé, Mengagdé.

mahasiddha (Skt.) One of great accomplishment, who has attained both the ordinary siddhis (miraculous powers) and the supreme siddhi (enlightenment).

Mahayana (Skt.) "Great Vehicle." The Mahayana teachings were first revealed by Arya Nagarjuna between the first and second century CE in South India. The legends say that Nagarjuna, who is sometimes called the "second Buddha," traveled to the realm of the nagas, or water serpents, and there retrieved the Mahayana teachings of Buddha that had been entrusted to the nagas' safekeeping until the world was ready to receive them.

These teachings were called the Great Vehicle (to enlightenment) because of the greatness of the aspirations of its followers, in contrast to that of the Hinayana, or "Lesser Vehicle." This great aspiration is characterized by the path of the bodhisattva, which has been described by E. A. Burtt: ". . . the bodhisattva has transcended the state in which he is concerned for his own salvation; he is committed to the eternal weal of all living beings, and will not rest until he has led them all to the goal. On attaining enlightenment he does not leave the world behind and enter nirvana by himself; he remains in the world, appearing like an ordinary person, but devoting his compassionate skill to the aid of others. He shares and bears the burden of their sufferings, in loving union with them, instead of merely giving others an example of a person who has overcome the causes of suffering for himself." (*The Teachings of the Compassionate Buddha*, p. 130)

For this reason the Mahayana is often called "the path of compassion." By following the path of the bodhisattva the goal of buddhahood, or full and total spiritual awakening, equal to that of the historical Buddha, can be attained.

Mahottara The Sanskrit name for Chemchok Heruka. *See* Chemchok Heruka.

Mara (Skt.) The demon who tried to tempt Buddha on the eve of his enlightenment. Mara is the evil lord of illusion who creates obstacles to enlightenment; he tries to distract spiritual practitioners and prevent them from progressing to enlightenment. Mara and his forces weave a web of illusion which makes samsara seem like a positive place and makes negative pastimes seem attractive. *See also* four maras.

Mengagdé (Tib.; Skt. *upadesha*) The Oral Instruction Class of Dzogchen teachings. There are four levels of Mengagdé: outer, inner, secret, and innermost secret. It is only within the Mengagdé that the highest levels of the Dharma are fully explicated and revealed; this is particularly true of the innermost secret level, where all of the most esoteric explanations and instructions of the ground, path, and fruition are completely explained. *See also* Semdé, Longdé.

mind terma treasure (Tib. *gongter*) A mind terma treasure is a category of terma discovered within the mind stream of the tertön. Dilgo Khyentsé Rinpoché writes, "Mind treasures arise in the following way: In many instances, after bestowing an empowerment or giving a teaching, Padmasambhava made the prayer, 'In the future, may this treasure arise in the mind of such and such tertön.' While doing so, he would focus his prayers and blessings on the tertön, usually an incarnation of one of his disciples. When, due to Guru Rinpoché's blessings, the time comes, both the words and the meaning of the treasure arise clearly in the tertön's mind. The tertön can then write these down without having to think." (*Brilliant Moon*, p. 141)

Nagarjuna (c.150–250) As one of the six great commentators (the "Six Ornaments") on the Buddha's teachings, the great scholar-alchemist-mahasiddha Nagarjuna is revered as an unsurpassed master by all Buddhist schools. His teachings provide the foundation for the Madhyamaka School, which propounds the "Middle Way" philosophy, accepted as the highest view within the sutra vehicle. He was also the revealer of the Prajnaparamita Sutras, the core teaching of the Mahayana, the second turning of the wheel of the Dharma. He is included among the Eighty-four Mahasiddhas, and among the Eight Vidyadharas.

nine yanas In the Early Translation tradition of the Nyingma School, the entire scope of Buddhist teachings is divided into nine progressive vehicles, or paths, presented according to the capacity and predisposition of the student.

The first three yanas—the paths of the shravaka, pratyekabuddha, and bodhisattva—are within the sutra tradition; the first two belong to the Hinayana, and the third to the Mahayana. The next six yanas are also Mahayana, and fall within the tantric tradition rather than the sutra tradition. The first three—kriyatantra, charyatantra, and yogatantra—are called the Outer Tantras. These emphasize Vedic asceticism. The second three—mahayogatantra, anuyogatantra, and atiyogatantra—are classified as the Inner Tantras. Here the emphasis is on powerful methods of skillful means.

Each progressive vehicle reveals and explains the teachings of the Buddha more fully, openly, and completely. The first eight yanas take ordinary mind (*sem*) as the path, whereas only the ninth, Atiyoga (or Dzogchen), considered the pinnacle of the nine yanas, takes rigpa as the path and not the ordinary mind.

The nine-yana method of classification was first mentioned in the scriptures of the Seventeen (or Eighteen) Dzogchen Tantras; in particular, they are referred to in *The All-Creating Monarch* (*Künjé Gyalpo*) and *The General Sutra of the Gathering of All Intentions* (*Dupa Do*).

nirmanakaya *See* four bodies of a buddha.

Nyingma (Tib.) The Nyingma or Nyingmapa (Ancient Ones) is the name given to the tradition of Tibetan Buddhism brought to Tibet by Guru Rinpoché Padmasambhava, with the support of King Trisong Detsen, and Abbot Shantarakshita. Also of particular importance in its establishment and spread were Yeshé Tsogyal, Vimalamitra, and Vairochana. It is also called the Early Translation School, as it comprised the first major round of translations of the Dharma into Tibetan.

nyingthig (Tib.) Literally, "heart essence." The term refers to the innermost secret level of the Mengagdé Class of Dzogchen instructions, which include the teachings of the extraordinary special preliminary practices of Dzogchen (*khordé rushen*), trekchö, and tögal, as well as the highest level of bardo teachings. They are the innermost essence of the essence.

Palden Lhamo (Tib.) *See* Remati.

pandita (Skt.) Scholar. *See* kusali.

pawo (Tib.) *See* daka.

pramana (Skt.) *See* valid cognition.

Pratimoksha (Skt.) Loosely translated as "personal liberation." The Pratimoksha vows originated with Shakyamuni Buddha and the monastic community, and are included within the Vinaya basket of teachings. They include the vows for monks and nuns, and also include certain vows for laypeople as well, such as the five lay precepts. Pratimoksha vows are held until one dies or breaks one of the four root vows.

primordial purity (Tib. *kadag*) The buddha nature, never tainted, that is present in all beings. Primordial purity is the source from which all the phenomena of samsara and nirvana appear.

Rahula (Skt.) "The sage of the Za (class)," he is a principal wrathful protector of the Nyingma terma tradition who seizes the sun and the moon and eclipses planets. Also known as "the eclipse maker," Rahula is green in color with nine heads and two hands, with his lower body that of a poisonous snake and his upper body that of a human.

rainbow body (Tib. *jalu ku*) The highest result of tögal practice, wherein the five ordinary elements of the physical body within oneself (earth, water, fire, air, and space) dissolve into their primordial form as light. Often all that remains are the hair and fingernails of the yogi/yogini. When one has accomplished the rainbow body one develops the capacity to continue to appear in various forms through endless time in order to help beings.

refuge One formally becomes a Buddhist when one takes refuge in the Three Jewels: the Buddha as the teacher or guide, the Dharma as the teachings or path, and the

Sangha as one's excellent companions on the journey. In tantra one adds taking refuge in the Three Roots: the guru as the root of all blessings, the yidam (or meditation deity) as the root of all attainments (or siddhis), and the dharmapalas, or protector deities (guardians), as the root of all enlightened activity.

Remati (Skt.; Tib. *Palden Lhamo*) Also called Revati, Namdru Remati, or Black Namdru. A name of Palden Lhamo, a form of Mahakali, and one of the main dharmapalas of all the major Tibetan lineages. Sometimes known as Lhamo Dusulma in the Pema Lingpa tradition, she is also described as the wrathful goddess of the twenty-seventh lunar mansion.

rigpa (Tib.; Skt. *vidya*) Intrinsic awareness. Rigpa is our buddha nature, a pure awareness that has been present since beginningless time. In Dzogchen, rigpa is the basis of the entire path. In Atiyoga, the master directly introduces the student to rigpa, evoking its indwelling essence to awaken in all its nakedness. Then once recognized, the student continues to practice this recognition again and again to gain certainty and confidence.

Rinpoché (Tib.) "Precious One." An honorific title reserved for tulkus or lamas of high rank or great meditative accomplishment.

sadhana (Skt.) The word *sadhana* literally means a way of accomplishing a specific result. It means a spiritual practice, usually a text of prayers, accompanied by visualization and mantra.

samadhi (Skt.; Tib. *samten*) Meditative absorption or concentration.

Samantabhadra (Skt.; Tib. *Kuntuzangpo*) The primordial dharmakaya buddha, representing our true nature of mind. He is represented as blue in color like the sky, naked indicating that he is awareness free from concepts, embracing his consort the female buddha Samantabhadri, who symbolizes emptiness, in yab-yum posture showing the union of awareness and emptiness.

samaya (Skt.; Tib. *damtsig*) The sacred vows and commitments related to the various yanas. At each level of entry into the Buddhist path there are specific commitments which one vows to uphold.

There is refuge ordination, the five lay precepts, the bodhisattva vow, monastic ordination, and tantra, and each stage has specific samayas. Also, when one receives tantric initiation from a vajra master into the mandala of a particular deity, one often receives a specific samaya associated with that practice.

In general, the samaya of the Hinayana is to cause no harm to any sentient beings; for the Mahayana the samaya is to help all sentient beings; for the Vajrayana the samaya is to retain sacred outlook. The most important samaya in tantra is to retain a pure relationship with one's guru.

In Dzogchen there are four samayas: two related to trekchö and two related to tögal. The trekchö samayas are nonexistence and all-pervasiveness. The two of tögal are spontaneous presence and oneness. These are also referred to as "the samayas that cannot be kept."

sambhogakaya (Skt.) Enjoyment body of a buddha. This is a body of light, a luminous energy form, and can only be seen by those who have accomplished a certain level of awakening. *See* four bodies of a buddha.

samsara (Skt.; Tib. *khorwa*) Cyclic existence, the wheel of life and death. The state of ordinary beings experiencing suffering and dissatisfaction in the six realms of transmigratory existence due to primordial ignorance. *See* six realms.

Sangha (Skt.) Sangha means the "excelled community." In the early days of Buddhism, the term was only applied to the ordained community of monks and nuns. It was later expanded to include lay disciples who had taken refuge in the Three Jewels: the Buddha, the Dharma, and the Sangha. In the Mahayana teachings, it can also be applied to include the Maha Sangha, or "great community," of all sentient beings, in much the same sense that Native Americans refer to the myriad forms of creation as "all my relations."

Sarasvati (Skt.; Tib. *Yangchenma*) "The one who gives the essence [or flow]." Sarasvati is the goddess of knowledge, music, the arts, and sciences. In Buddhism she is the consort of Manjushri, the bodhisattva of wisdom. She is also praised as Loter Yangchenma, the second emanation of the Twenty-one Taras; Loter means "giver of knowledge," and Yangchenma means "she who is the source of melodies." Sarasvati is often depicted as a beautiful woman holding a vina (Indian lute). In addition to her place in the Buddhist pantheon, Sarasvati is worshipped in Hinduism, Jainism, and Zoroastrianism.

Sarma (Tib.) Sarma means the New, or Later, Translation Schools of Tibetan Buddhism. These took place after the grandson of King Trisong Detsen, Langdarma, who was loyal to the Bön religion of his mother, killed his brother, the reigning king Tri Ralpalchen, and established himself as king. Once he gained rule, he persecuted the Buddhist Sangha for years until only three monks and a handful of white-robed tantrikas were left to keep the tradition alive. Eventually Langdarma was himself assassinated by Lhalung Pelgyé Dorjé, whereupon the lineage of kings ended and the Dharma waned.

Later, Atisha was invited to Tibet to help reestablish the Dharma. Many subsequent translators after Atisha, such as Marpa Lotsawa, brought the scriptures back from India. All the subsequent schools and lineages to emerge were known as the Sarma schools. These include the Kagyu, Gelug, and Sakya Schools, the main traditions surviving today.

Semdé (Tib.) The Mind Class cycle of Dzogchen teachings. According to the great Dzogchen master Chögyal Namkhai Norbu, "In Semde, the 'mind series,' the practitioner is introduced to the nature of mind in order to have a concrete experience of it." (From www.tashigarnorte.org/eng/dzochen4.html). *See also* Longdé, Mengagdé.

Seventeen Tantras The essential tantras of the Mengagdé Oral Instruction (*upadesha*) Class of Dzogchen. Said to be a revelation of Garab Dorjé, the Seventeen Tantras were brought to Tibet by Padmasambhava and Vimalamitra. They mainly contain the pith instructions Nyingthig instructions for trekchö and tögal. They are sometimes enumerated as the Eighteen Tantras or Nineteen Tantras. According to the Rigpa Wiki: "The tradition of Vimalamitra adds to them the *Tantra of the Wrathful Mother, Protectress of Mantras [Ekajati]* (*ngak sung tröma*) to make eighteen in all, while the tradition of Padmasambhava also arrives at a total of eighteen by adding the *Tantra of the Blazing Expanse of Luminosity [of Samantabhadri]* (*longsal barma*). Generally, however, both the *Tantra of the Wrathful Mother, Protectress of Mantras* from Vimalamitra's tradition and the *Tantra of the Blazing Expanse of Luminosity* from Padmasambhava's tradition are added to the Seventeen Tantras of the Innermost Secret Nyingtik Cycle, making a total of nineteen altogether."

shedra (Tib.) "Place of learning." A shedra is a Buddhist school with a program of study thoroughly introducing the fundamental teachings of the three yanas. It is usually attended by monks, and more recently nuns, in their teens and twenties, and is roughly equivalent to secondary school and college. Not all monks and nuns attend a shedra. Some go on to higher postgraduate studies and attain the degree of khenpo or geshé, the titles varying according to the different lineages. More recently shedras have opened up to Westerners and laypeople; there are even distant learning online shedra studies available in Western languages.

siddha (Skt.) One who has attained siddhis. *See* siddhi.

siddhi (Skt.; Tib. *ngodrup*) Attainment, accomplishment, spiritual powers. There are two levels of siddhi: ordinary and supreme. The ordinary, or common, siddhis are the psychic powers and abilities that occur as a result of meditation practice; these include such miraculous abilities as levitation, flying, invisibility, the ability to create multiple images of oneself and appear in different places at the same time, or to change form. The extraordinary siddhis refer to spiritual realization, the signs of the perfection of wisdom and compassion.

six extraordinary qualities of Samantabhadra The six extraordinary features of the liberation of Samantabhadra are also called the six special dharmas of Dzogchen. In his book, *Guru Yoga* (page 92), Dilgo Khyentse Rinpoche describes these as follows:

1. This liberation arises to our own awareness as the display of this awareness. There are no deluded perceptions that come from clinging to this display as an outer phenomenon.
2. This liberation transcends the aspects of "primordial ground" and "manifestation that arises from the primordial ground." If not, there would be a possibility of falling into delusion as phenomena arise from the primordial ground.
3. If we recognize the primordial wisdom free from all obscurations, at that very instant all the qualities that dwell naturally within the expanse of that wisdom spontaneously appear. We realize that the obscurations related to the various karmic tendencies accumulated upon the amorphous basic consciousness are pure from the very beginning. Like a brilliant sun emerging from the clouds, we transcend utterly the ground of samsara.
4. At the same instant, transcendent insight matures as the kaya of the ultimate nature itself; we conquer the citadel of primordial purity and dwell there immutably.
5. The actualization of our own awareness is not born from outer circumstances provided by something other than awareness itself, and it is independent of all conditions. Buddhahood is achieved through awareness recognizing its own nature, through its own strength.
6. The ground for liberation dwells primordially in the continuum of its own nature, and cannot be penetrated by the causes of delusion.

six lamps The six lamps are a further description of awareness and its appearances as they arise in tögal practice: (1) the abiding lamp of the ground; (2) the chitta flesh lamp of the heart; (3) the smooth white channel lamp; (4) the lamp of the far-reaching watery lasso; (5) the pure lamp of the expanse; (6) the bardo lamp of time. *See* four lamps.

Six Ornaments and Two Supreme Ones The Six Ornaments are the six great commentators on the teachings of the Buddha: Nagarjuna, Aryadeva, Asanga, Vasubandhu, Dignaga, and Dharmakirti. The Two Supreme Ones are Gunaprabha and Shakyaprabha.

six paramitas Also known as the six perfections or six transcendent virtues. Cultivation of the six paramitas is the basis of the Mahayana, the path of the bodhisattva.

The six paramitas are: generosity, ethics or moral discipline, patience, joyous effort, meditative concentration, and wisdom.

six realms The six dimensions of samsaric existence are: the god (*deva*) realm, brought about by pride; (2) the fighting or jealous god (*asura*) realm, brought about by jealousy or envy; (3) the human realm, brought about by desire; (4) the animal realm, brought about by ignorance and stupidity; (5) the hungry ghost (*preta*) realm, brought about by greed; and (6) the hell realm, brought about by hatred and anger. The first three are known as the upper realms of samsara, and the last three are known as the lower realms. *See* Desire Realm, Form Realm, Formless Realm.

skandha (Skt.) Literally, "heap." Often translated as "aggregate," it means a gathering of parts. In the Buddhist context it refers to the various mental and physical component parts that make up what we call a human being. There are five main parts, called "the five skandhas." These are: (1) form, (2) feeling/sensations, (3) perception, (4) choice, and (5) consciousness.

sloka (Skt.) A verse or stanza.

Sogdrubma (Tib.) "Butcheress Life Protectress." Also called Shenpa Sogdrubma. A female Dharma protector.

spontaneous presence (Tib. *lhündrup*) The appearances of the ground of primordial purity. Within Dzogchen a distinction is made between the ground itself (the youthful vase body) and the ground manifesting as appearances through the "eight doorways of spontaneous presence." This accounts for all of the perceptions, both pure and impure, that arise within the mind. In his work *The Precious Treasury of the Supreme Vehicle*, Longchenpa describes spontaneous presence as follows: "Having broken the shell of the youthful vase body, the primordial ground of the originally pure inner ultimate sphere, by the flow of the prana of primordial wisdom, the self-appearances of rigpa flash out from the ground as the eight spontaneously accomplished doors.

"As everything is spontaneously arisen from the appearances of the eight spontaneously accomplished doors, it is called the 'great simultaneously arising of the appearances of samsara and nirvana.' When the appearances spontaneously arise from the inner radiance as the outer radiance, the appearances of their essence are self-clarity, which is the space of unobstructedness, the appearances of their nature are the natural glow as the five lights, and the appearances of compassion are the aspect of providing the cloudless sky-like space. (This is the arising of the appearances of the ground from the ground.)

"When the appearances of the ground arise, phenomenal existents arise as lights and kayas (buddha bodies). It is called the appearances of everything as the spontaneously accomplished [buddha] field. From the power of the essence of that field arise the appearances of sambhogakaya, from the power of their qualities arise the appearances of svabhavanirmanakaya, and from their power of compassion arise the aspects of samsara, like dreams." (From Tulku Thondup, *The Practice of Dzogchen*, pp. 206-207)

The eight spontaneously accomplished doors are: (1) compassion, 2) light, (3) kayas, (4) primordial wisdom (*yeshé*), (5) nonduality, (6) freedom from extremes, (7) the impure gate of samsara, and (8) the pure gate of primordial wisdom. For a detailed description of the eight spontaneously accomplished doors, see Tulku Thondup, *The Practice of Dzogchen*, p. 206, n. 1.

tantra (Skt.; Tib. *gyü*) Literally, "thread" or "continuum." Tantra generally refers to the fundamental texts of the Vajrayana, and to the systems of meditation described therein. In the Nyingma tradition of the nine yanas, the tantras are classified according to six levels, with the divisions being defined according to class of scriptures as well as the view and emphasis in practice. First there are the three outer tantras: Action (kriya), Performance (charya), and Union (yogatantra); then there are the three inner tantras: Great Union (mahayoga), Further (anuyoga), and Utmost (Atiyoga). Tantra works on simultaneously transforming the three aspects of one's ordinary body, speech, and mind into the transcendent body, speech, and mind of a buddha through mudra, mantra, and meditation.

Because of its many skillful methods of practice, tantric Buddhism is often called "the short path" to awakening. Through tantra it is possible to attain complete buddhahood in one lifetime, as compared to the many aeons of effort required through Hinayana and the sutra levels of Mahayana practice.

Tibetan medicine and astrology are also presented in scriptures called tantras.

tantrika (Skt.) One who is practicing tantra.

Tara (Skt.; Tib. *Drölma*) A female bodhisattva-goddess said to have been born from a tear in Avalokiteshvara's eye as he asked for a helper to aid in the liberation of all sentient beings. Tara manifests in twenty-one different forms to help beings.

Three Jewels (Skt. *triratna*; Tib. *könchog sum*) The three objects of refuge in all forms of Buddhism are: the Buddha, or awakened teacher; the Dharma, or teachings; and the Sangha, or community of fellow practitioners. These three form the essential foundation for successful spiritual practice.

Three Roots In addition to taking refuge in the Three Jewels, in Vajrayana the practitioner also takes refuge in the Three Roots: the guru as the root of all blessings, the yidam as the root of all siddhis, and the Dharma protectors as the root of all enlightened activities.

ten virtuous actions Also called the ten wholesome actions, these are the opposite of the ten nonvirtuous actions: (1) not to kill, but to cherish all life; (2) not to take what is not given, but to respect the things of others; (3) not to engage in harmful sexuality, but to be caring and responsible and to respect the vows, rights, and commitments of others; (4) not to lie, but to speak the truth; (5) not to engage in idle chatter and gossip, but to speak meaningfully and constructively; (6) not to speak of the faults of others, but to be understanding and sympathetic; (7) not to praise oneself and disparage others, but to overcome one's own shortcomings; (8) not to covet that which belongs to others, but to rejoice in the happiness, wealth, and success of others; (9) not to indulge in anger or hatred nor to wish harm upon others, but to practice forbearance; (10) not to revile the Three Jewels, nor to hold wrong views, but to cherish and uphold the Three Jewels.

terma (Tib.) Sacred objects, texts, or teachings hidden by Padmasambhava and Yeshé Tsogyal, and other great masters such as Longchenpa, as time capsules for the benefit of beings in later times when the termas are prophesied to be found. The masters who discover terma are called "tertöns," treasure finders. Terma are mainly of two types: earth treasures and mind treasures. Earth termas are found in physical locations, such as caves or cemeteries; and in elements such as water, wood, earth, or space. Mind termas are received in dreams, visionary experience, or found directly in the deep levels of consciousness of the tertön. *See also* earth terma, mind terma, tertön.

tertön (Tib.) Treasure finder. *See* terma.

tögal (Tib.; Skt. *vyutkrantaka*) Translated variously as "leaping over," "crossing over," "direct crossing," or "surpassing the pinnacle." Often referred to as *lhündrup tögal*, "leaping over to spontaneous presence," tögal is the highest of practices in Dzogchen and in all the nine yanas. Tögal belongs to the innermost, or quintessential, secret class of Mengagdé. It is unique to Dzogchen and is not found in the other yanas.

In tögal practice, by receiving the ripening empowerment and liberating instructions from the lama, and through striking the key points of the special postures and gazes, one directly engages with the clear light appearances that are spontaneously present and manifesting as direct perception of rigpa's radiance, originating in one's own heart. By means of the four lamps or six lamps, the four visions arise, and culminate in buddhahood. The highest signs of tögal attainment are the rainbow body or the body of great transference.

torma (Tib.) Literally, "a cast out thing," a torma is a sculpted offering made of colored barley flour and butter used in tantric rituals as an offering, or propitiation, to various spiritual beings. There are also deity tormas, representing particular yidams or protectors.

trekchö (Tib.) One of the two innermost secret practices of Dzogchen. Translated as "cutting through" or "breakthrough." Often referred to as *kadag trekchö*, "cutting through to primordial purity." What one cuts through are ignorance, fixation, grasping, attachment, and dualistic perception. Trekchö practice reveals the experience of the primordial purity of emptiness, the youthful vase body. *See* youthful vase body.

trikaya (Skt.) The three kayas, or three bodies of a buddha: the dharmakaya, sambhogakaya, and nirmanakaya.

tulku (Tib.; Skt. *nirmanakaya*) Incarnate lamas who have voluntarily taken rebirth in fulfillment of their bodhisattva vows to help beings. The power to determine one's rebirth is gained upon attainment of the eighth stage of awakening of a bodhisattva.

Vaishravana (Skt.; Tib. *Nam Tö Sé*, also known as *Jambhala* or *Dzambhala*) He is a Dharma protector of the Buddha's teachings, and particularly of those who are upholding the Vinaya precepts of moral discipline. He also dons golden armor and protects the gods from the *asuras*, or demigods. The highest of the Four Great Guardian Kings, he is the directional protector of the North and king of the *yakshas*. His name means "Son of He Who Has Heard Many Things." Vaishravana is also a wealth guardian who grants both worldly and spiritual wealth to practitioners. He is often depicted as gold or ruby in color, holding in his right hand a red-bannered lance, and in his left hand holding a mongoose who is emitting jewels from its mouth, symbolizing the attribute of conferring wealth.

vajra (Skt.; Tib. *dorjé*) Indestructible, diamondlike, adamantine, thunderbolt. A ritual scepter used in Vajrayana practice. It symbolizes skillful means and compassion, the masculine aspect of enlightened activity. The vajra is diamondlike in that it is clear, priceless, and indestructible, symbolizing the qualities of the highest truth, unborn and undying.

Vajrasattva (Skt.; Tib. *Dorjé Sempa*) Appearing in sambhogakaya form, Vajrasattva embodies the one hundred peaceful and wrathful deities. Meditation on Vajrasattva is one of the principal practices for purification. In Dzogchen he is the main sambhogakaya buddha.

Vajravarahi (Skt.; Tib. *Dorjé Phagmo*) Vajravarahi, or "Diamond Sow," one of the forms of Vajrayogini, is considered the root of all dakinis, and is a central yidam in all the main lineages, including Nyingma, Kagyu, Gelug, and Sakya. She is usually depicted as red in color, with a small crying sow's head protruding from her own head over her ear, representing the buddha family of Vairochana and the transformation of ignorance and passion into dharmadhatu wisdom and compassion.

Vajrayana (Skt.) Diamond Vehicle.

Vajrayogini (Skt.; Tib. *Dorjé Naljorma*) A semiwrathful female yidam. Red in color, with one face and two arms, she holds an upraised hook knife (Tib. *driguk*) in her right hand and a skull cup full of blood in her left hand. She wears a skull crown and bone ornaments. Her symbolic meaning is the same as Vajravarahi. In some traditions, such as the Kagyu, she is the first yidam used as an introduction to the practice of tantra.

valid cognition (Skt. *pramana*) The term "valid cognition" is a translation of *pramana* ("sources of knowledge"), an epistemological term in Hindu and Buddhist dialectic, debate, and discourse. It can also be translated as "knowing things as they are." It is related to subject, object, and action, and to how things are knowable.

vidyadhara (Skt.; Tib. *rigdzin*) Awareness or knowledge (*vidya*) holder (*dhara*). It refers to one who has attained the ability to remain or hold constantly in the state of awareness.

Vinaya (Skt.) One of the "Three Baskets" (*Tripitaka*) of the Buddhist scriptures, the Vinaya deals with Buddhist ethics and rules of conduct governing the life of the Sangha. The bulk of the Vinaya pertains to monks and nuns, but it also contains precepts, teachings, and advice for laypeople.

yaksha (Skt.) A class of nature spirits that are keepers of treasure hidden in the earth or in the roots of trees.

yana (Skt.) Literally, "vehicle." The term implies a means of conveyance that will carry us along on the path. The three main vehicles are the "Small Vehicle," or Hinayana, which is compared to a bicycle as it focuses on the relatively smaller goal of individual liberation; the "Great Vehicle," or Mahayana, which is compared to a bus as it focuses on the vast altruistic motivation of a bodhisattva, who chooses to forego complete departure from the confused existence of samsara, but rather to stay and help until all beings are liberated; and the "Diamond Vehicle," or Vajrayana, a division of Mahayana compared to a diamond for its clarity, strength, and priceless qualities as it is quick, effective, and contains many methods to suit the varied needs and capacities of its different followers. These three are further subdivided into the nine yanas as defined by the Nyingma system.

yidam (Tib.) One of the Three Roots, a yidam is the personal meditation deity of a Vajrayana practitioner. Although some yidams are prescribed and taught to everyone within a particular lineage at a preliminary level, the guru will later select a specific yidam for each practitioner in accordance with one's karmic connections and particular afflictions.

As a preliminary to yidam practice, one must be accomplished in guru yoga and have great faith and devotion to the guru. This enables the practitioner to identify with the lineage and to establish a deep inner connection with the yidam. In this way one can transform the energy of one's neurosis into its enlightened expression, as represented by the yidam. Identification with the yidam also cuts through deeply entrenched attachment to one's ordinary body, speech, and mind.

yogi, yogin (Skt.; Tib. *naljorpa*) A male tantric practitioner. In Tibet the term *yogi* is often used to contrast a lay practitioner from an ordained monk. Also, since *yogi* can sometimes mean someone who is practicing the higher yogas, which ultimately means someone taking on a sexual consort, the term *yogi* is sometimes used to designate married lamas and practitioners, in contrast to celibate monks. In its general sense, however, a yogi is anyone who practices yoga, so a monk can also be called a *yogi*.

yogini (Skt.; Tib. *naljorma*) A female tantric yoga practitioner.

youthful vase body (Tib. *zhönnu bumpai ku*) A poetic name and metaphor for the inner radiance of emptiness, signifying the nondual oneness of the dharmakaya, where all qualities are timeless, pure, pristine, unborn, and undying (youthful); present but not yet manifest, as if enclosed within a vase.

BIBLIOGRAPHY

Burtt, E. A., ed. and comm. *The Teachings of the Compassionate Buddha.* New York: New American Library, 1955.

Dilgo Khyentse. *Brilliant Moon.* Boston: Shambhala, 2008.

———. *Guru Yoga: According to the Preliminary Practice of Longchen Nyingtik.* Translated by Matthieu Ricard and edited by Rigpa. Ithaca: Snow Lion Publications, 1999.

Dowman, Keith, trans. and comm. *The Legend of the Great Stupa and the Life Story of the Lotus Born Guru.* Berkeley: Tibetan Nyingma Meditation Center, 1973.

Dudjom Rinpoche. *The Nyingma School of Tibetan Buddhism: Its Fundamentals and History.* 2 vols. Translated and edited by Gyurme Dorje and Matthew Kapstein. Boston: Wisdom Publications, 1991.

Fremantle, Francesca. *Luminous Emptiness: Understanding the* Tibetan Book of the Dead. Boston: Shambhala, 2001.

Harding, Sarah, trans. *The Life and Revelations of Pema Lingpa.* Ithaca: Snow Lion Publications, 2003.

Jigmed Lingpa, Vidyādhara. *Yeshe Lama.* Translated by Lama Chönam and Sangye Khandro. Ithaca: Snow Lion Publications, 2008.

Karma Thinley. *The History of the Sixteen Karmapas of Tibet.* Boulder: Prajñā Press, 1980.

Kunsang, Erik Pema, comp. and trans. *Wellsprings of the Great Perfection: Lives and Insights of the Early Masters in the Dzogchen Lineage.* Boudanath, Hong Kong, and Esby: Rangjung Yeshe Publications, 2006.

Longchen Rabjam. *The Practice of Dzogchen* [previously published as *Buddha Mind: An Anthology of Longchen Rabjam's Writings on Dzogpa Chenpo*]. Translated by Tulku Thondup; edited by Harold Talbott. Ithaca: Snow Lion Publications, 2002.

Longchenpa. *Kindly Bent to Ease Us.* 3 vols. Translated and annotated by Herbert V. Guenther. Berkeley: Dharma Publishing, 1975-76.

———. *You Are the Eyes of the World.* Translated by Kennard Lipman and Merrill Peterson. Ithaca: Snow Lion Publications, 2010.

Namdrol Rinpoche, Khenpo. *The Three Statements that Strike the Vital Point: The Last Testament of Prahevajra (Garab Dorje)*. Translated by Sangye Khandro, the Light of Berotsana Translation Group. Light of Berotsana Translation Group, 2007.

Namkhai Norbu. *The Crystal and the Way of Light: Sutra, Tantra, and Dzogchen*. Compiled and edited by John Shane. Ithaca: Snow Lion Publications, 2000.

———. *The Dzogchen Ritual Practices*. Edited and translated by Brian Beresford, assisted by Judith Allan and Lindsay Young. London: Kailash Editions, 1991.

Nyoshul Khenpo. *A Marvelous Garland of Rare Gems: Biographies of Masters of Awareness in the Dzogchen Lineage*. Junction City, Calif.: Padma Publishing, 2005.

Patrul Rinpoche. *The Words of My Perfect Teacher*. Boston: Shambhala, 1998.

Shenga, Khenpo. *In Praise of Longchenpa*. Translated by Adam Pearcey. Lotsawa House (www.lotsawahouse.org).

Stewart, Jampa Mackenzie. *The Life of Gampopa*. Ithaca: Snow Lion Publications, 2002.

Tenzin Gyatso, His Holiness the Dalai Lama. *Dzogchen: The Heart Essence of the Great Perfection*. Translated by Geshe Thupten Jinpa and Richard Barron and edited by Patrick Gaffney. Ithaca: Snow Lion Publications, 2000.

———. *Mind in Comfort and Ease: The Vision of Enlightenment in the Great Perfection*. Translated by Matthieu Ricard, Richard Barron, and Adam Pearcey. Boston: Wisdom Publications, 2007.

Trulshik Adeu Rinpoche and Tulku Urgyen Rinpoche. *Skillful Grace: Tara Practice for Our Times*. Translated by Erik Pema Kunsang; edited by Marcia Binder Schmidt. Boudanath, Hong Kong, and Esby: Rangjung Yeshe Publications, 2007.

Tulku Thondup. *Masters of Meditation and Miracles: The Longchen Nyingthig Lineage of Tibetan Buddhism*. Edited by Harold Talbott. Boston: Shambhala, 1996.

Tulku Urgyen Rinpoche. *Vajra Speech: Pith Instructions for the Dzogchen Yogi*. Translated by Erik Pema Kunsang; compiled by Marcia Binder Schmidt; and edited by Michael Tweed. Boudanath, Hong Kong, and Esby: Rangjung Yeshe Publications, 2001.

Yangthang Tulku. *The Nyingthig Yabshi Empowerments*. Translated by Sangye Khandro. Mt. Shasta, Calif.: Yeshe Melong Publications, 1990.

ENGLISH TRANSLATIONS OF
LONGCHENPA'S WRITINGS

Dowman, Keith, comp. and comm. *Maya Yoga: Longchenpa's Finding Comfort and Ease in Enchantment. A Book of Dzogchen Precepts.* Kathmandu: Vajra Books, 2010.

———, trans. and comm. *Natural Perfection: Longchenpa's Radical Dzogchen* [originally published as *Old Man Basking in the Sun.* Kathmandu: Vajra Books, 2006]. Boston: Wisdom Publications, 2010.

Klong-chen rab-'byams-pa. *Looking Deeper: A Swan's Questions and Answers.* Translated and annotated by Herbert V. Guenther. Porthill, Idaho: Timeless Books, 1983.

Longchen Rabjam. *The Four-Themed Precious Garland: An Introduction to Dzogchen*, with commentaries by Dudjom Rinpoche and Beru Khyentse Rinpoche. Translated by Alexander Berzin. Dharamsala: Library of Tibetan Works and Archives, 1978.

———. *The Practice of Dzogchen* [originally published as *Buddha Mind: An Anthology of Longchen Rabjam's Writings on Dzogpa Chenpo*]. Translated by Tulku Thondup. Ithaca: Snow Lion Publications, 2002.

———. *The Precious Treasury of the Basic Space of Phenomena* [*Chöying Dzö*]. Translated by Richard Barron. Junction City, Calif.: Padma Publishing, 2001.

———. *The Precious Treasury of Philosophical Systems* [*Drupta Dzö*]. Translated by Richard Barron. Junction City, Calif.: Padma Publishing, 2007.

———. *The Precious Treasury of Pith Instructions* [*Mengag Dzö*]. Translated by Richard Barron. Junction City, Calif.: Padma Publishing, 2006.

———. *The Precious Treasury of the Way of Abiding* [*Nelug Dzö*] and *The Exposition of the Quintessential Meaning of the Three Categories: A Commentary on the Precious Treasury of the Way of Abiding* [*Desum Nyingpo Döndrel Nelug Rinpoché Dzö Jé Chaway Drelpa*]. Translated by Richard Barron. Junction City, Calif.: Padma Publishing, 1998.

———. *Thorough Dispelling of Darkness throughout the Ten Directions* [*Drelwa Chogchu Münsel*]. In Lama Chönam and Sangye Khandro, trans., *The Guhyagarbha*

Tantra: Secret Essence Definitive Nature Just As It Is. Ithaca: Snow Lion Publications, 2011.

———. *A Treasure Trove of Scriptural Transmission: A Commentary on* The Precious Treasury of the Basic Space of Phenomena [*Lungki Ter Dzö*]. Translated by Richard Barron. Junction City, Calif.: Padma Publishing, 2001.

Longchenpa. *Kindly Bent to Ease Us.* [*Ngalso Korsum*]. Translated and annotated by Herbert V. Guenther. 3 vols. Berkeley: Dharma Publishing, 1975-76.

———. *Now That I Come to Die* [*Zhalchen Nekyi Melong*]. Translated by Herbert V. Guenther and the Yeshe De Translation Group. Berkeley: Dharma Publishing, 2007.

———. *A Visionary Journey.* Translated and annotated by Herbert V. Guenther. Boston: Shambhala, 1989.

———. *You Are the Eyes of the World.* [*Kun Ché Gyalpo*] Translated by Kennard Lipman and Merrill Peterson, with introduction by Namkhai Norbu. Ithaca: Snow Lion Publications, 2010.

Namkhai Norbu, Chögyal. *Longchenpa's Advice from the Heart,* with commentary by Chögyal Namkhai Norbu. Conway, Mass.: Shang Shung Publications, 2008.

Tenzin Gyatso, His Holiness the Dalai Lama. *Mind in Comfort and Ease: The Vision of Enlightenment in the Great Perfection.* Translated by Matthieu Ricard, Richard Barron, and Adam Pearcey. Boston: Wisdom Publications, 2007.

CREDITS

The translation of *In Praise of Longchen Rabjam* by Khenpo Shenga. Used with permission from Adam Pearcey, Rigpa Translations.

Excerpts from *The Legend of the Great Stupa and the Life Story of the Lotus Born Guru*, © 1973 Tibetan Nyingma Meditation Center. Used with permission from Dharma Publishing, shop.dharmapublishing.com.

Excerpts from *The Life and Revelations of Pema Lingpa*, © 2003 Sarah Harding. Used with permission from Shambhala Publications, www.shambhala.com.

Excerpts from *A Marvelous Garland of Rare Gems: Biographies of Masters of Awareness in the Dzogchen Lineage*, © 2005 Padma Publishing. Used with permission from Padma Publishing, tibetantreasures.com/Books-Padma_Publishing.html.

Excerpts from *Masters of Meditation and Miracles: The Longchen Nyingthig Lineage of Tibetan Buddhism*, © 1996 Tulku Thondup. Used with permission from Shambhala Publications, www.shambhala.com.

Excerpts from *The Nyingma School of Tibetan Buddhism: Its Fundamentals and History*, © 1991 Dudjom Rinpoche, Gyurme Dorje, and Matthew Kapstein. Used with permission from Wisdom Publications, www.wisdompubs.org.

Excerpts from transcripts of *The Nyingtik Yabshi Empowerments*, given by the Venerable Yangthang Rinpoche, San Francisco, 1990. Used with permission from Vimala Treasures, vimalatreasures.org.

Excerpts from *The Oral Construction of Exile Life and Times of Künkhyen Longchen Rabjam in Bumthang* by Dorji Penjore. Used with permission from Dorji Penjore.

Excerpts from *The Practice of Dzogchen* (originally published as *Buddha Mind*), © 1989, 1996, and 2002 Tulku Thondup. Used with permission from Shambhala Publications, www.shambhala.com.

Excerpts from *Wellsprings of the Great Perfection: Lives and Insights of the Early Masters in the Dzogchen Lineage*, © 2006 Erik Hein Schmidt. Used with permission from Rangjung Yeshe Publications, www.rangjung.com.

INDEX

<small>DHARMA PROTECTORS OF THE DZOGCHEN LINEAGE</small>
Top row, left to right: Za Rahula, Dorjé Legpa
Center: Manin Nagpo, the neutral-gender head of the Mahakala family
Bottom row, left to right: Ekajati, Remati Palden Lhamo